English Grammar

For International Communication

30 Lessons
with Examples
Exercises and
Vocabulary

Gramática Inglesa

Para La Comunicación Internacional

30 LECCIONES
CON EJEMPLOS
EJERCICIOS Y
VOCABULARIO

Prof. Benjamin Franklin Arias, Ph.D.

©Copyright 2018 Benjamín Franklin Arias, Ph.D.
Registrado en 1998 con el Numero 000467 Libro 01
en la Oficina Nacional de Derechos de Autor de la República Dominicana,
de acuerdo con lo establecido en la Ley 32-86.
E-mail: benfrank1305@gmail.com

Información sobre impresión disponible en la última página.

ISBN: 978-1-4907-8990-3 (sc)
ISBN: 978-1-4907-8992-7 (e)

Library of Congress Control Number: 2018953463

Trafford rev. 09/09/2022

Trafford
PUBLISHING®   www.trafford.com
Para Norteamérica y el mundo entero
llamadas sin cargo: 844-688-6899 (USA & Canadá)
fax: 812 355 4082

English Grammar

For International Communication

30 Lessons
with Examples
Exercises and
Vocabulary

Gramática Inglesa

Para La Comunicación Internacional

30 LECCIONES
CON EJEMPLOS
EJERCICIOS Y
VOCABULARIO

Prof. Benjamin Franklin Arias, Ph.D.

DEDICATORIA

A todos los Estudiantes y Profesores de Inglés...
A las Instituciones Educativas que me han empleado...
A quienes me han ayudado en las senda de mi desarrollo
Intelectual y Espiritual...
A mis inolvidables amigos...
Entre ellos a Nerys Pacheco y Pascual Estrella...
A todos mis familiares...
A mis seres más queridos:
A mi Padre, Rafael Arias
A mi Madre, Venecia Lara
A mis Hermanos y Hermanas.
Y especialmente...

A mis Hijos con todo mi Amor.

Prof. Benjamin Franklin Arias, Ph.D.

AGRADECIMIENTO

En primer lugar, agradezco a Dios por darme el don de la vida, la salud y la inteligencia suficiente para aprender y poder compartir mis conocimientos con mis semejantes. Así mismo, agradezco a todas las personas que me motivaron y me estimularon para seguir adelante en la realización de este humilde libro. Y también, agradezco profundamente, a quienes, de una manera u otra, colaboraron grandemente para hacer posible su publicación. Y, como muestra de nuestro mayor afecto y agradecimiento, se lo dedicamos en toda su extensión.

Prof. Benjamin Franklin Arias, Ph.D.

CONTENIDO

Dedicatoria vii

Agradecimiento ix

Introducción xix

PRIMERA PARTE
Puntos Gramaticales Y Ejercicios

Lección 1 **The Indefinite Article** — El Artículo Indefinido 4

           Ejercicio 1 5

Lección 2 **Plural Form** — Formación Del Plural 8

           Ejercicio 2 10

Lección 3 **This, These, That, Those** — Esto, Estos, Eso, Esos 12

           Ejercicio 3 13

           Ejercicio 4 14

           Ejercicio 5 15

Lección 4 **Verb To Be; Affirmative Form**—Verbo Ser, Estar;
Forma Afirmativa 18

        Verb To Be; Contractions In Affirmative Form—
Verbo Ser, Estar; Contracciones En La Forma Afirmativa. . . 18

           Ejercicio 6 19

        Verb To Be; Question Form—Verbo Ser, Estar; Forma
Interrogativa 20

           Ejercicio 7 21

Lección 5 **Verb To Be; Negative Form**—Verbo Ser, Estar; Forma
Negativa 24

           Ejercicio 8 25

        Verb To Be; Contractions In Negative Form—Verbo
Ser, Estar; Contracciones En La Forma Negativa 27

           Ejercicio 9 28

Lección 6 **There Is, There Are**—Hay (Singular Y Plural) 32

           Ejercicio 10 33

Lección 7   **Verb To Have; Affirmative Form**—Verbo Tener; Forma
Afirmativa 36

Ejercicio 11 37

Lección 8   **Verb To Have; Question Form**—Verbo Tener; Forma
Interrogativa. 40

Verb To Have; Negative Form—Verbo Tener; Forma
Negativa. 40

Ejercicio 12 41

Lección 9   **Simple Present Tense; Affirmative Form**—Tiempo
Presente Simple; Forma Afirmativa 46

Ejercicio 13 48

Present Tense; Question Form—Tiempo Presente;
Forma Interrogativa. 49

Ejercicio 14 50

Present Tense; Negative Form—Tiempo Presente;
Forma Negativa. 52

Ejercicio 15 53

Lección 10   **Possessive Adjectives** — Adjetivos Posesivos. 56

Ejercicio 16 57

Lección 11   **Have To; Affirmative Form**—Tener Que; Forma Afirmativa . 60

Have To; Negative Form—Tener Que; Forma Negativa . . . 60

Ejercicio 17 61

Lección 12   **Personal Pronouns; Objective Case**—Pronombres
Personales; Caso Acusativo 66

Ejercicio 18 67

Lección 13   **Imperative Form**—Forma Imperativa 70

Ejercicio 19 71

Lección 14   **Present Progressive**—Presente Progresivo 74

Ejercicio 20 75

Lección 15   **Verb To Be; Past Tense**—Verbo Ser, Estar; Tiempo Pasado . 78

Ejercicio 21 79

Lección 16   **Past Progressive**—Pasado Progresivo. 82

Ejercicio 22 83

Lección 17   **Past Tense Of Regular Verbs**—Tiempo Pasado De
Verbos Regulares. 86

Past Tense Of Irregular Verbs—Tiempo Pasado De
Verbos Irregulares 87

Ejercicio 23 88

Lección 18 **Auxiliary Did**—Auxiliar Did 90

Ejercicio 24 91

Auxiliary Can—Auxiliar Can (Poder) 93

Auxilary Could—Auxiliar Could (Pudo, Podria) 93

Auxiliary May—Auxliliar May (Poder) 94

Auxiliary Must—Auxiliar Must (Deber) 94

Auxiliary Should—Auxiliar Should (Deberia) 95

Auxiliary Would—Auxiliar Would 95

Auxiliary Verbs; Question Form—Verbos Auxiliares,
Forma Interrogativa 96

Ejercicio 25 97

Auxiliary Verbs; Negative Form—Verbos Auxiliares;
Forma Negativa 99

Ejercicio 26 100

Lección 19 **Future Tense Using Will And Going To**—Tiempo
Futuro Usando Will Y Going To 104

Ejercicio 27 105

Lección 20 **Information Questions Using What**—Preguntas
Informativas Usando What (Que) 110

Information Questions Using Where—Preguntas
Informativas Usando Where (Donde) 111

Information Questions Using When—Preguntas
Informativas Usando When (Cuando) 112

Information Questions Using How—Preguntas
Informativas Usando How (Como) 113

Information Questions Using Why—Preguntas
Informativas Usando Why (Por Que) 114

Ejercicio 28 115

Lección 21 **Information Questions Using How Many**—Preguntas
Informativas Usando How Many (Cuantos, Cuantas) 118

Information Questions Using How Much—
Preguntas Informativas Usando How Much (Cuanto,
Que Cantidad) 119

Ejercicio 29 120

Lección 22 **Adjectives—Adverbs**—Adjetivos—Adverbios 122

    Ejercicio 30 123

    Adjectives; Comparative Degree—Adjetivos; Grado
    Comparativo. 124

    Ejercicio 31 125

    Adjectives; Superlative Degree—Adjetivos; Grado
    Superlativo. 126

    Ejercicio 32 127

Lección 23 **Some, Any**—Algunos, Ningunos 130

    Ejercicio 33 131

Lección 24 **Very, Too**—Muy, Demasiado 134

    Ejercicio 34 135

Lección 25 **Possessive Pronouns**—Pronombres Posesivos 138

    Ejercicio 35 139

Lección 26 **Reflexive Pronouns**—Pronombres Reflexivos. 142

    Ejercicio 36 143

Lección 27 **Present Perfect Tense; Affirmative Form**—Tiempo
    Presente Perfecto; Forma Afirmativa 146

    Ejercicio 37 148

    Present Perfect Tense; Question Form—Tiempo
    Presente Perfecto; Forma Interrogativa 149

    Present Perfect Tense; Negative Form—Tiempo
    Presente Perfecto; Forma Negativa 150

    Ejercicio 38 151

Lección 28 **Past Perfect Tense**—Tiempo Pasado Perfecto 156

    Ejercicio 39 158

Lección 29 **Passive Voice**—Voz Pasiva 160

    Ejercicio 40 161

Lección 30 **Conditional Sentences—Future Possible**—
    Oraciones Condicionales—Futuro Posible. 164

    Conditional Sentences—Present Unreal—
    Oraciones Condicionales—Presente Irreal 164

    Conditional Sentences—Past Unreal—Oraciones
    Condicionales—Pasado Irrea. 165

    Ejercicio 41 166

    Ejercicio 42 168

SEGUNDA PARTE

Respuestas A Los Ejercicios

Ejercicio 1 173
Ejercicio 2 173
Ejercicio 3 174
Ejercicio 4 174
Ejercicio 5 175
Ejercicio 6 175
Ejercicio 7 176
Ejercicio 8 177
Ejercicio 9 178
Ejercicio 10 179
Ejercicio 11 179
Ejercicio 12 180
Ejercicio 13 181
Ejercicio 14 181
Ejercicio 15 182
Ejercicio 16 182
Ejercicio 17 183
Ejercicio 18 184
Ejercicio 19 185
Ejercicio 20 186
Ejercicio 21 186
Ejercicio 22 187
Ejercicio 23 187
Ejercicio 24 188
Ejercicio 25 189
Ejercicio 26 190
Ejercicio 27 191
Ejercicio 28 192
Ejercicio 29 192

Ejercicio 30 193

Ejercicio 31 193

Ejercicio 32 194

Ejercicio 33 194

Ejercicio 34 195

Ejercicio 35 195

Ejercicio 36 196

Ejercicio 37 196

Ejercicio 38 197

Ejercicio 39 198

Ejercicio 40 198

Ejercicio 41 199

Ejercicio 42 199

TERCERA PARTE

Temas Misceláneos

---

1. **Definite Article**—Articulo Definido. 205

2. **Contractions**—Contracciones 207

3. **Adverbs Of Mode**—Adverbios De Modo 210

4. **Adverbs Of Place**—Adverbios De Lugar 211

5. **Adverbs Of Quantity**—Adverbios De Cantidad 211

6. **Adverbs Of Time**— Adverbios De Tiempo 212

7. **Conjunctions**—Conjunciones .213

8. **Interjections**—Interjecciones .214

9. **Prepositions**—Preposiciones. .215

10. **Cardinal Numbers**—Numeros Cardinales 216

11. **Ordinal Numbers**—Numeros Ordinales 218

12. **Colors**—Colores 219

13. **Days Of The Week**—Dias De La Semana. 219

14. **Months Of The Year**—Meses Del Año 220

15. **Seasons Of The Year**—Estaciones Del Año. 220

CUARTA PARTE
Verbos

1. **Regular Verbs**—Verbos Regulares. 225
2. **Irregular Verbs**—Verbos Irregulares. 239

QUINTA PARTE
Vocabulario

1. **Vocabulary**—Vocabulario 247
2. **Proper Nouns**—Nombres Propios 289

Bibliografia 293
Otros Libros Del Autor 297

INTRODUCCIÓN

INTRODUCCIÓN

El idioma Inglés es conocido como el idioma internacional por excelencia. Es tanto el uso que se le da, que podemos notar su extraordinaria influencia en todos los aspectos de la vida diaria en todo el mundo. Lo usamos en los estudios, los deportes, los viajes, los negocios... Otro ejemplo notable es que, en esta nueva era de grandes avances científicos y tecnológicos, se hace muy necesario el dominio de este importante idioma para el uso correcto de los sistemas computarizados. Por lo tanto, podemos afirmar que en todos los pueblos y países del mundo hay una reconocida y notable cantidad de habitantes que, con seguridad, entiende, habla, lee y escribe en inglés.

Como cualquier otro idioma, el inglés tiene sus reglas o su gramática, y un correcto conocimiento práctico de esas reglas permite que nos comuniquemos correctamente en todos los niveles académicos y sociales. Es precisamente esto lo que ofrecemos en este libro: Un selecto conjunto de reglas gramaticales, con el claro objetivo de que, después de su estudio y práctica, pueda el estudiante o profesor alcanzar un dominio básico de la GRAMATICA INGLESA y pueda demostrarlo al hacer uso de este idioma oralmente o por escrito.

Hemos diseñado este libro dividiéndolo en cinco partes, las cuales detallamos a continuación. En la PRIMERA PARTE, presentamos, primeramente, los puntos gramaticales que hemos seleccionado y que consideramos de mayor importancia. Estos están acompañados de breves explicaciones para facilitar el aprendizaje. Luego, se dan ejemplos traducidos al español, en los que se usan esas reglas gramaticales. Y, para un aprendizaje más permanente, ofrecemos por último, los ejercicios en los que deben aplicarse las reglas o puntos ya presentados, explicados y usados en ejemplos.

En la SEGUNDA PARTE, puedes encontrar las respuestas a todos los ejercicios. Estas pueden ser usadas para la auto evaluación o para la aclaración en caso de que se haga un poco difícil al tratar de responder o completar algunas partes de los ejercicios.

En la TERCERA PARTE, ofrecemos una variedad de temas misceláneos, que incluye listados de palabras correspondientes a diversos puntos gramaticales de uso frecuente, así como diferentes vocabularios clasificados por temas, que resultan útiles y necesarios para una buena comunicación.

En las CURTA PARTE, hemos colocado una interesante selección de verbos regulares e irregulares. Estos últimos dados con el pasado y participio pasado correspondientes.

Y en la QUINTA PARTE, que consideramos de mucha importancia, damos el vocabulario completo de todas las palabras que hemos usado en este libro, sin incluir los cambios o transformaciones que pueden darse en cada una de ellas. Este vocabulario es de mucha utilidad, ya que pueden aparecer algunas palabras desconocidas al momento en que se hacen los ejercicios presentados en la PRIMERA PARTE. Después de éste, también damos en orden alfabético, los nombres propios que hemos usado.

No esta demás agregar, que la BIBLIOGRAFIA, dada al final del libro, puede ser aprovechada para seguir profundizando el conocimiento del idioma Inglés. Por lo tanto, recomendamos, si existe la posibilidad, que también estudie y coloque en su biblioteca los libros indicados, y que también hemos consultado para la realización de éste.

Esperamos que esta entrega que hacemos a los profesores y estudiantes de inglés de aquí y de todas partes, pueda ayudarles a usar correctamente este idioma. Y de esto estamos seguros, si cada día se aparta un tiempo considerable para estudiar y poner en práctica regularmente las enseñanzas de este libro, el cual hemos preparado con el fin de que se pueda dominar y usar la GRAMATICA INGLESA PARA LA COMUNICACION INTERNACIONAL.

PROF. BENJAMIN FRANKLIN ARIAS, AUTOR.

English Grammar

For International Communication

Gramática Inglesa

Para La Comunicación Internacional

Prof. Benjamin Franklin Arias, Ph.D.

PRIMERA PARTE

Puntos Gramaticales Y Ejercicios

LESSON 1

◆ The Indefinite Article

THE INDEFINITE ARTICLE

EL ARTICULO INDEFINIDO

El artículo indefinido es **A** (un, una) el cual se usa delante de palabras que empiezan con consonante y **AN** (un, una) delante de palabras que empiezan con sonido vocal. En este caso se incluye la **H** muda.

A teacher	un profesor
A student	un estudiante
A mechanic	un mecánico
An example	un ejemplo
An exercise	un ejercicio
An hour	una hora
A friend	un amigo
A dog	un perro
An elephant	un elefante
An orange	una naranja

EJERCICIO 1   COMPLETA CON A O AN

E. _____A_____ book.

1. _____ student.

2. _____ apple.

3. _____ banana.

4. _____ umbrella.

5. _____ orange.

6. _____ horse.

7. _____ elephant.

8. _____ egg.

9. _____ month.

10. _____ article.

11. _____ friend.

12. _____ idea.

13. _____ house.

14. _____ car.

15. _____ island.

16. _____ easy exercise.

17. _____ difficult exercise.

18. _____ big house.

19. _____ interesting lesson.

20. _____ nice girl.

LESSON 2

♦ Plural Form

PLURAL FORM

FORMACION DEL PLURAL

La mayoría de los nombres en inglés forman su plural al agregarse una **S** al singular.

A chair	una silla
Some chairs	algunas sillas
A table	una mesa
Some tables	algunas mesas
A book	un libro
Some books	algunos libros
A pen	un lapicero
Some pens	algunos lapiceros

Los nombres que terminan en **CH, S, O, SH, X** se les agrega **ES** para formar el plural.

Church	iglesia
Churches	iglesias
Bus	autobús
Buses	autobuses
Tomato	tomate
Tomatoes	tomates
Dish	plato
Dishes	platos
Box	caja
Boxes	cajas

Si terminan en **Y** después de consonante se cambia por **I** y se agrega **ES**

City	ciudad
Cities	ciudades
Secretary	secretaria
Secretaries	secretarias

Si terminan en **Y** después de vocal se agrega **S** solamente.

Boy	muchacho
Boys	muchachos
Toy	juguete
Toys	juguetes

IRREGULAR PLURAL FORM

FORMA DEL PLURAL IRREGULAR

Algunos nombres en inglés tienen una forma especial o irregular para cambiar al plural.

Man	hombre
Men	hombres
Woman	mujer
Women	mujeres
Foot	pie
Feet	pies
Child	niño
Children	niños
Tooth	diente
Teeth	dientes
Mouse	ratón
Mice	ratones
Person	persona
People	personas

EJERCICIO 2   CAMBIA AL PLURAL

E   Chair   Chairs

1. Table   _____

2   Porch   _____

3. Box   _____

4. Book   _____

5. Boss   _____

6. Pen   _____

7. Man   _____

8. Foot   _____

9. Tomato   _____

10. Bus   _____

11. Kiss   _____

12. Church   _____

13. Woman   _____

14. Child   _____

15. Tooth   _____

16. Teacher   _____

17. House   _____

18. Mouse   _____

19. Potato   _____

20. Lesson   _____

LESSON 3

- ◆ This
- ◆ These
- ◆ That
- ◆ Those

THIS, THESE, THAT, THOSE

ESTO, ESTOS, ESO, ESOS

Se usa **THIS** para referirse a algo que está cerca de nosotros. Se usa **THAT** para referirse a algo que esta lejos. **THESE** es el plural de **THIS** y **THOSE** de **THAT**.

1.	This chair is green.	Esta silla es verde.
2.	This book is blue.	Este libro es azul.
3.	What is this?	¿Qué es esto?
4.	This is a box.	Esta es una caja.
5.	That is a church.	Esa es una iglesia.
6.	These chairs are blue.	Estas sillas son azules.
7.	These pens are black.	Estos lapiceros son negros.
8.	What are those?	¿Qué son esos?
9.	Those are pencils.	Esos son lapices.
10.	Those tables are yellow.	Esas mesas son amarillas.

EJERCICIO 3　　　　　COMPLETA CON THIS O THESE

E	_____This_____	pen
1.	_____	picture
2.	_____	page
3.	_____	words
4.	_____	flower
5.	_____	people
6.	_____	classes
7.	_____	store
8.	_____	erasers
9.	_____	car
10.	_____	church
11.	_____	books
12.	_____	dish
13.	_____	women
14.	_____	child
15.	_____	weather
16.	_____	pens
17.	_____	coats
18.	_____	money
19.	_____	boxes
20.	_____	baby

EJERCICIO 4   COMPLETA CON THAT O THOSE

E   _____Those_____   coats

1. _____   boy

2. _____   doctors

3. _____   girls

4. _____   women

5. _____   box

6. _____   language

7. _____   radio

8. _____   children

9. _____   money

10. _____   students

11. _____   word

12. _____   books

13. _____   man

14. _____   baby

15. _____   chairs

16. _____   ladies

17. _____   dress

18. _____   class

19. _____   tables

20. _____   pen

EJERCICIO 5   CAMBIA AL PLURAL

E   This book   _____ These books _____

1.   This pen   _____

2.   That table   _____

3.   This pencil   _____

4.   That school   _____

5.   This page   _____

6.   This car   _____

7.   That man   _____

8.   This house   _____

9.   That picture   _____

10.   That woman   _____

11.   This child   _____

12.   This class   _____

13.   That word   _____

14.   That store   _____

15.   That dress   _____

16.   This lesson   _____

17.   That student   _____

18.   That box   _____

19.   This country   _____

20.   That question   _____

LESSON 4

- ♦ To Be
- ♦ Affirmative Form
- ♦ Question Form

VERB TO BE; AFFIRMATIVE FORM

VERBO SER, ESTAR ; FORMA AFIRMATIVA

I am	Yo soy, estoy
You are	Tú eres, estás
He is	El es, está
She is	Ella es, está
It is	Es, esta (animal o cosa)
We are	Nosotros somos, estamos
You are	Ustedes son, están
They are	Ellos son, están

1.	I am a teacher.	Yo soy un profesor.
2.	You are a student.	Tú eres un estudiante.
3.	He is a mechanic.	El es un mecánico.
4.	She is a nurse.	Ella es una enfermera.
5.	It is a dog.	Es un perro.
6.	We are professionals.	Nosotros somos profesionales.
7.	You are students.	Ustedes son estudiantes.
8.	They are teachers.	Ellos son profesores.

VERB TO BE; CONTRACTIONS IN AFFIRMATIVE FORM

VERBO SER, ESTAR; CONTRACCIONES EN LA FORMA AFIRMATIVA.

I'm
You're
He's
She's
It's
We're
You're
They're

EJERCICIO 6   COMPLETA CON AM, IS, ARE

E. He _____ is _____ a teacher.

1. I _____ a student.

2. Frank _____ a doctor.

3. This _____ a good book.

4. Kathy and Mary _____ good friends.

5. We _____ good students.

6. Mr. Arias _____ a teacher.

7. He _____ a good dentist.

8. Miss Rodriguez _____ a beautiful girl.

9. She _____ a secretary.

10. You _____ a good waiter.

11. Helen and Suzan _____ good waitresses.

12. They _____ sisters.

13. The windows _____ open.

14. The door _____ closed.

15. Today _____ Monday.

16. This _____ a good exercise.

17. These _____ my books.

18. They _____ brothers.

19. I _____ very busy today.

20. You and Henry _____ teachers.

VERB TO BE; QUESTION FORM

VERBO SER, ESTAR; FORMA INTERROGATIVA

La forma interrogativa del verbo **TO BE** se hace colocando el verbo (**AM**, **IS**, **ARE**) al principio de la oración.

1.	Am I a teacher? *	¿Soy un profesor?
2.	Are you a student?	¿Eres un estudiante?
3.	Is he a mechanic?	¿Es él un mecánico
4.	Is she a nurse?	¿Es ella una enfermera?
5.	Is it a dog?	¿Es un perro?
6.	Are we professionals?	¿Somos profesionales?
7.	Are you students?	¿Son ustedes estudiantes?
8.	Are they teachers?	¿Son ellos profesores?

* El pronombre personal **I** (Yo) se escribe siempre en mayúscula.

EJERCICIO 7 CAMBIA A LA FORMA INTERROGATIVA

E. I am a teacher.

Am I a teacher?

1. You are a student.

   _____

2. He is a mechanic.

   _____

3. She is a nurse.

   _____

4. It is a dog.

   _____

5. We are professionals.

   _____

6. You are students.

   _____

7. They are teachers.

   _____

8. We are cousins.

   _____

9. He is a bad student.

   _____

10. Today is Tuesday.

   _____

11. John and Christopher are in the same class.

   _____

12. You and George are cousins.

   _____

13. She and Mary are good friends.

   _____

14. The door is open.

   _____

15. The window is closed.

   _____

16. They are new students.

   _____

17. We are busy today.

   _____

18. Mr. Smith and Mrs. White are Americans.

   _____

19. This is a difficult exercise.

   _____

20. That is a good book.

   _____

LESSON 5

- ♦ To Be
- ♦ Negative Form
- ♦ Contractions In Negative Form

VERB TO BE; NEGATIVE FORM

VERBO SER, ESTAR; FORMA NEGATIVA

La forma negativa del verbo **TO BE** se hace colocando **NOT** después del verbo (**AM, IS, ARE**).

1.	I am not a student.	No soy un estudiante.
2.	You are not a teacher.	Tú no eres un profesor.
3.	He is not a pilot.	El no es un piloto.
4.	She is not a secretary.	Ella no es una secretaria.
5.	It is not a cat.	No es un gato.
6.	We are not mechanics.	Nosotros no somos mecánicos.
7.	You are not lawyers.	Ustedes no son abogados.
8.	They are not policemen.	Ellos no son policías.

EJERCICIO 8   CAMBIA A LA FORMA NEGATIVA

E.   I am a student.

    <u>I am not a student.</u>

1.   You are a teacher.

    _____

2.   He is a pilot.

    _____

3.   She is a secretary.

    _____

4.   It is a car.

    _____

5.   We are mechanics.

    _____

6.   You are lawyers.

    _____

7.   They are policemen.

    _____

8.   He is happy.

    _____

9.   She is pretty.

    _____

10. You are from Europe.

    _____

11. Mary is very happy.

   _____

12. They are ready now.

   _____

13. The boy is small.

   _____

14. The house is big.

   _____

15. They are students here.

   _____

16. Mr. Brown is busy now.

   _____

17. English is very difficult.

   _____

18. Mary and Helen are students.

   _____

19. This English book is expensive.

   _____

20. The children are in the house.

   _____

VERB TO BE; CONTRACTIONS IN NEGATIVE FORM

VERBO SER, ESTAR; CONTRACCIONES EN LA FORMA NEGATIVA

1.	I'm not a student.	No soy un estudiante.
2.	You aren't a teacher.	Tú no eres un profesor.
3.	He isn't a pilot.	El no es un piloto.
4.	She isn't a secretary.	Ella no es una secretaria.
5.	It isn't a cat.	No es un gato.
6.	We aren't mechanics.	No somos mecánicos.
7.	You aren't lawyers.	Ustedes no son abogados.
8.	They aren't policemen.	Ellos no son policías.

EJERCICIO 9

HAGA CONTRACCIONES EN LA FORMA NEGATIVA

E. We are not brothers.

   <u>We aren't brothers.</u>

1. Today is not Monday.

   _____

2. She and Mary are not sisters.

   _____

3. This is not a difficult exercise.

   _____

4. He is not a good student.

   _____

5. Mr. Lara is not a good teacher.

   _____

6. Peter and John are not Americans.

   _____

7. She is not a good friend.

   _____

8. They are not busy today.

   _____

9. You and Henry are not cousins.

   _____

10. Joseph and I are not in the same class.

   _____

11. William is not busy today.

_____

12. You are not a good student.

_____

13. You and George are not good friends.

_____

14. Mary and I are not good friends.

_____

15. The door is not closed.

_____

16. The blue windows are not open.

_____

17. They are not brothers.

_____

18. We are not friends.

_____

19. They are not new students.

_____

20. He is not a good doctor.

_____

LESSON 6

- ◆ There Is
- ◆ There Are

THERE IS; THERE ARE

HAY (singular y plural)

Estas son frases importantes en inglés y corresponden en el español a **HAY**. En el singular se usa **THERE IS** y en plural **THERE ARE**. Para la forma negativa e interrogativa siguen las reglas del verbo **TO BE**.

1.	There is a book on the table.	Hay un libro en las mesa.
2.	Is there a pen near the book?	¿Hay un lapicero cerca del libro?
3.	There isn't a pen near the book.	No hay un lapicero cerca del libro.
4.	There are five chairs in this room.	Hay cinco sillas en este cuarto.
5.	Are there two tables in the dining room?	¿Hay dos mesas en el comedor?
6.	There aren't two tables in the dining room.	No hay dos mesas en el comedor.

EJERCICIO 10

COMPLETA CON THERE IS O THERE ARE

E. _____There is_____ a magazine on the chair.

1. _____ two men in the office.

2. _____ many children in the park.

3. _____ a man at the door.

4. _____ many people on the bus.

5. _____ seven days in a week.

6. _____ twelve months in a year.

7. _____ a rug on the floor.

8. _____ two windows in this room.

9. _____ many students in our class.

10. _____ only one chair in this room.

11. _____ several pictures on the wall.

12. _____ only one cloud in the sky.

13. _____ three dishes on the table.

14. _____ many churches in this city.

15. _____ four women in the office.

16. _____ nobody in the room.

17. _____ somebody at the door.

18. _____ many new words in this lesson.

19. _____ a new student in our class.

20. _____ a letter for you here.

LESSON 7

- ♦ To Have
- ♦ Affirmative Form

VERB TO HAVE; AFFIRMATIVE FORM

VERBO TENER; FORMA AFIRMATIVA

I have	Yo tengo
You have	Tú tienes
He has	El tiene
She has	Ella tiene
It has	Tiene (animal o cosa)
We have	Nosotros tenemos
You have	Ustedes tienen
They have	Ellos tienen

1. I have a blue book. — Yo tengo un libro azul.
2. You have a red pen. — Tú tienes un lapicero rojo.
3. He has a big family. — Él tiene una familia grande.
4. She has a car. — Ella tiene un carro.
5. The dog has a small plate. — El perro tiene un plato pequeño.
6. We have a round table. — Tenemos una mesa redonda.
7. You have a large library. — Ustedes tienen una biblioteca grande.
8. They have a green house. — Ellos tienen una casa verde.

Nota: Los adjetivos calificativos se usan antes de los nombres.

EJERCICIO 11   COMPLETA CON HAVE O HAS

E.   I _____have_____ a blue book.

1.   You _____ a red pen.

2.   She _____ a car.

3.   He _____ a big family.

4.   The dog _____ a short tail.

5.   We _____ a round table.

6.   You _____ a large library.

7.   They _____ a green house.

8.   Helen _____ a new hat.

9.   I _____ many good friends.

10.   We _____ new English books.

11.   You _____ a good pen.

12.   The cat _____ a long tail.

13.   This book _____ a blue cover.

14.   I _____ a new book.

15.   Mary _____ a new dress.

16.   Benjamin _____ a very good watch.

17.   Franklin and Erik _____ many good friends.

18.   We _____ some pencils but no pens.

19.   I _____ two sisters and four brothers.

20.   Benny _____ a new computer.

LESSON 8

- ♦ To Have
- ♦ Question Form
- ♦ Negative Form

VERB TO HAVE; QUESTION FORM

VERBO TENER; FORMA INTERROGATIVA

1.	Do I have a book?	¿Tengo un libro?
2.	Do you have a pen?	¿Tienes un lapicero?
3.	Does he have a big family?	¿Tiene él una familia grande?
4.	Does she have a car?	¿Tiene ella un carro?
5.	Does the dog have a plate?	¿Tiene el perro un plato?
6.	Do we have a table?	¿Tenemos una mesa?
7.	Do you have a library?	¿Tienen ustedes una biblioteca?
8.	Do they have a green house?	¿Tienen ellos una casa verde?

VERB TO HAVE; NEGATIVE FORM

VERBO TENER; FORMA NEGATIVA

1.	I don't have a book.	No tengo un libro.
2.	You don't have a pen.	No tienes un lapicero.
3.	He doesn't have a big family	El no tiene una familia grande.
4.	She doesn't have a car.	Ella no tiene un carro.
5.	The dog doesn't have a plate.	El perro no tiene un plato.
6.	We don't have a table.	No tenemos una mesa.
7.	You don't have a library.	Ustedes no tienen una biblioteca.
8.	They don't have a green house.	Ellos no tienen una casa verde.

Nota: En las formas INTERROGATIVA y NEGATIVA se usa HAVE con todas las personas o pronombres.

EJERCICIO 12 — CAMBIA A LA FORMA INTERROGATIVA Y CONTESTA EN LA FORMA NEGATIVA

E. He has a pen.

Does he have a pen?

No, he doesn't have a pen.

1. She has many friends in our class.

2. You have a new pen.

3. He has three English classes a week.

4. They have a new car.

5. We have a good time at the party.

6. John has an English class every day.

7. They have their vacation in July.

   _____

   _____

8. She has two brothers and one sister.

   _____

   _____

9. We have many new words to learn today.

   _____

   _____

10. Helen has a new hat.

    _____

    _____

11. You have a red shirt.

    _____

    _____

12. We have our English class in Room 5.

    _____

    _____

13. She has a bad cold.

    _____

    _____

14. Frank has a headache.

    _____

    _____

15. They have a new television set.

    _____

    _____

16. We have many friends in New York.

    _____

    _____

17. That dog has a very long tail.

    _____

    _____

18. The teacher has brown hair.

    _____

    _____

19. This book has a blue cover.

    _____

    _____

20. He has many English books.

    _____

    _____

LESSON 9

- ◆ Simple Present Tense
- ◆ Affirmative Form
- ◆ Question Form
- ◆ Negative Form

SIMPLE PRESENT TENSE; AFFIRMATIVE FORM

TIEMPO PRESENTE SIMPLE; FORMA AFIRMATIVA

a) El tiempo presente simple de todos los verbos en inglés, con excepción del verbo **TO BE**, tiene la misma forma que el infinitivo. Sin embargo, en la tercera forma del singular (**he, she, it**) se agrega una **S**. Se usa este tiempo para describir una acción que ocurre cada día o en general.

To work	**Trabajar**
I work	Yo trabajo
You work	Tú trabajas
He works	El trabaja
She works	Ella trabaja
It works	Trabaja, funciona
We work	Nosotros trabajamos
You work	Ustedes trabajan
They work	Ellos trabajan

b) En la tercera persona singular (**he, she, it**) los verbos que terminan en la letra **Y** seguida de una consonante se cambia la **Y** por **I** y se agrega **ES**.

To study	**Estudiar**
I study	Yo estudio
You study	Tú estudias
He studies	El estudia
She studies	Ella estudia
We study	Nosotros estudiamos
You study	Ustedes estudian
They study	Ellos estudian

c) Los verbos que terminan en **O, S, CH, SH, X** se les agrega **ES** en la tercera persona del singular (**he, she, it**).

To go	**Ir**
I go	Yo voy
You go	Tú vas
He goes	El va
She goes	Ella va
It goes	Va
We go	Nosotros vamos
You go	Ustedes van
They go	Ellos van

To kiss	**Besar**
(He, she, it) kisses	besa

To wash	**lavar**
(He, she, it) washes	lava

To watch	**Mirar**
(He, she, it) watches	mira

To fix	**Arreglar**
(He, she, it) fixes	arregla

Prof. Benjamin Franklin Arias, Ph.D.

EJERCICIO 13	COMPLETA CON LA FORMA CORRECTA DEL TIEMPO PRESENTE

E.   (speak) He _____speaks_____ English very well

1.   (write) We _____ many letters.

2.   (go) She _____ to school every day.

3.   (sit) I always _____ in this seat.

4.   (open) John always _____ the windows for the teacher.

5.   (work) Mr. Lopez _____ in this room.

6.   (smoke) He _____ many cigarettes.

7.   (kiss) She _____ her boyfriend every day.

8.   (read) They _____ the newspaper every day.

9.   (eat) She _____ in the cafeteria every day.

10. (play) We _____ tennis every afternoon.

11. (wash) He _____ his clothes every week.

12. (carry) She _____ her books in a briefcase.

13. (try) I always _____ to come to school on time.

14. (study) Frank _____ English every night.

15. (put) She _____ her pens on the desk.

16. (watch) Mary _____ T.V. every night.

17. (bring) They _____ notebooks to the class.

18. (fix) He often _____ his watch when it doesn't work.

19. (prepare) We always _____ our homework every day.

20. (leave) The train _____ at eight o'clock.

48

PRESENT TENSE; QUESTION FORM

TIEMPO PRESENTE; FORMA INTERROGATIVA

Para hacer la forma interrogativa con los verbos en presente, se usa **DO** con **I, you, we, they**. Se usa **DOES** con **he, she, it** y a los verbos se le quita la terminación de **S** o **ES**.

To travel	**Viajar**
Do I travel?	¿Viajo?
Do you travel?	¿Viajas?
Does he travel?	¿Viaja (él)?
Does she travel?	¿Viaja (ella)?
Does it travel?	¿Viaja?
Do we travel?	¿Viajamos?
Do you travel?	¿Viajan (ustedes)?
Do they travel?	¿Viajan (ellos)?

To wash	**Lavar**
Do I wash?	¿Lavo?
Do you wash?	¿Lavas?
Does he wash?	¿Lava el?
Does she wash?	¿Lava ella?
Does it wash?	¿Lava?
Do we wash?	¿Lavamos?
Do you wash?	¿Lavan ustedes?
Do they wash?	¿Lavan ellos?

EJERCICIO 14	CAMBIA A LA FORMA INTERROGATIVA. USA DO O DOES

E.   They like coffee.

<u>Do they like coffee?</u>

1.   The boy knows the answer.

_____

2.   The girls work in a store.

_____

3.   You know many new words.

_____

4.   John studies very hard.

_____

5.   They go to school every day.

_____

6.   She asks many questions.

_____

7.   We spend a lot of money.

_____

8.   Mr. Arias speaks very fast.

_____

9.   You understand the lesson.

_____

10.   They write many letters.

_____

11. He knows many English words.

_____

12. Mary speaks English very well.

_____

13. The boys like coffee.

_____

14. The women come from Canada

_____

15. Mr. Brown teaches English.

_____

16. Helen lives in New York.

_____

17. That student studies every day.

_____

18. The baby cries very much.

_____

19. He writes letters every day.

_____

20. They go to Mexico every year.

_____

PRESENT TENSE; NEGATIVE FORM

TIEMPO PRESENTE; FORMA NEGATIVA

Para hacer la forma negativa con los verbos en presente, se usa **DON'T (DO NOT)** con **I, you, we, they**; se usa **DOESN'T (DOES NOT)** con **he, she, it** y a los verbos se le verbos se le quita la terminación **S** o **ES**.

To work	**Trabajar**
I don't work	Yo no trabajo
You don't work	Tú no trabajas
He doesn't work	El no trabaja
She doesn't work	Ella no trabaja
It doesn't work	No trabaja
We don't work	Nosotros no trabajamos
You don't work	Ustedes no trabajan
They don't work	Ellos no trabajan

EJERCICIO 15 — CAMBIA A LA FORMA NEGATIVA. USA DON'T O DOESN'T

E.   I know that word.

I don't know that word.

1.   He understands that lesson.

2.   They go to school every day.

3.   She asks many questions.

4.   Frank writes many letters.

5.   The men come from Brazil.

6.   The tall woman speaks very fast.

7.   That boy works very hard.

8.   I study the lesson every day.

9.   Those people like coffee.

10. They speak French well.

11. Those boys live in Chicago.

   _____

12. Mr. Smith teaches English.

   _____

13. We know many English words.

   _____

14. John and William have many friends.

   _____

15. They spend a lot of money.

   _____

16. She studies every afternoon.

   _____

17. He speaks that language.

   _____

18. Mr. Brown works very hard.

   _____

19. The new students understand this.

   _____

20. Mr. Lopez flies to England every year.

   _____

LESSON 10

◆ Possessive Adjectives

POSSESSIVE ADJECTIVES

ADJETIVOS POSESIVOS

I	My	mi, mis
You	Your	su, sus (de usted)
He	His	su, sus (de él)
She	Her	su, sus (de ella)
It	Its	su, sus (de animal o cosa)
We	Our	nuestro, nuestra, nuestros, nuestras
You	Your	su, sus, (de ustedes)
They	Their	su, sus (de ellos)

1. My book is blue.   Mi libro es azul.
2. Your house is green.   Su casa es verde.
3. His car is black.   Su carro es negro.
4. Her children are in Canada. Sus niños están en Canada
5. Its puppies are white.   Sus cachorros son blancos.
6. Our country is beautiful.   Nuestro país es hermoso.
7. Your books are yellow.   Sus libros son amarillos.
8. Their cars are new.   Sus carros son nuevos.

EJERCICIO 16

COMPLETA CON MY, YOUR, HIS, HER, ITS, OUR, THEIR

E   I drink _____my_____ juice.

1.   The boy walks to _____ chair.

2.   The girl walks to _____ chair.

3.   I walk to _____ chair.

4.   We study _____ lessons every night.

5.   I put _____ book on the desk.

6.   She likes _____ English class.

7.   We bring _____ books to class.

8.   Franklin and Enmanuel bring _____ books to class.

9.   The girls bring _____ pencils to the university.

10.   Our teacher, Benjamin, comes to school in _____ car.

11.   Peter studies English in _____ room.

12.   I study in _____ room.

13.   The dog chases _____ tail.

14.   The cat eats _____ dinner.

15.   I often look at _____ watch during the lesson.

16.   Mary, our teacher, often looks at _____ watch during the lesson.

17.   Many of the students look at _____ watches during the lesson.

18.   You write many words in _____ notebook every day.

19.   Benny and Erik play with _____ toys.

20.   We always prepare _____ homework every day.

LESSON 11

- ◆ Have to
- ◆ Affirmative Form
- ◆ Negative Form

HAVE TO; AFFIRMATIVE FORM

TENER QUE; FORMA AFIRMATIVA

1. I have to come early. — Tengo que venir temprano.
2. You have to go to the hospital. — Tú tienes que ir al hospital.
3. He has to eat more. — El tiene que comer más.
4. She has to dance with me. — Ella tiene que bailar conmigo.
5. It has to be at three o'clock. — Tiene que ser a las tres en punto.
6. We have to speak English. — Tenemos que hablar Inglés.
7. You have to write sentences. — Tienen que escribir oraciones.
8. They have to eat bananas. — Ellos tienen que comer guineos.
9. Frank has to come tomorrow. — Frank tiene que venir mañana.
10. Lisa has to go to the hospital. — Lisa tiene que ir al hospital.

HAVE TO; NEGATIVE FORM

TENER QUE; FORMA NEGATIVA

1. I don't have to come early. — No tengo que venir temprano.
2. You don't have to go to the hospital. — Tú no tienes que ir al hospital.
3. He doesn't have to eat more. — El no tiene que comer más.
4. She doesn't have to dance with me. — Ella no tiene que bailar conmigo.
5. It doesn't have to be at three o'clock. — No tiene que ser a las tres en punto.
6. We don't have to speak Spanish. — No tenemos que hablar español.
7. You don't have to write sentences. — Ustedes no tienen que escribir oraciones.
8. They don't have to eat bananas. — Ellos no tienen que comer guineos.
9. Frank doesn't have to come tomorrow. — Frank no tiene que venir mañana.
10. Lisa doesn't have to go to the hospital. — Lisa no tiene que ir al hospital.

EJERCICIO 17

**USA HAVE TO O HAS TO
EN LA FORMA AFIRMATIVA
Y DON'T O DOESN'T HAVE TO
EN LA FORMA NEGATIVA**

E.   I come early every day.

I have to come early every day.

I don't have to come early every day.

1.   You go to the hospital.

_____

_____

2.   He eats more.

_____

_____

3.   She dances with me.

_____

_____

4.   It is at three o'clock

_____

_____

5.   We speak English.

_____

_____

6.   You write sentences.

_____

_____

7. They eat bananas.

    _____

    _____

8. Kathy comes to class every day.

    _____

    _____

9. Lisa goes to the hospital.

    _____

    _____

10. She writes many letters.

    _____

    _____

11. He buys many books.

    _____

    _____

12. I read the newspaper every morning.

    _____

    _____

13. She drinks milk with her meals.

    _____

    _____

14. He eats lunch in the cafeteria.

    _____

    _____

15. I get up early every morning.

_____

_____

16. They speak English in Canada.

_____

_____

17. She comes to school by bus.

_____

_____

18. We speak Spanish every day.

_____

_____

19. He eats dinner at home.

_____

_____

20. They read many English books.

_____

_____

LESSON 12

- ♦ Personal Pronouns
- ♦ Objective Case

PERSONAL PRONOUNS; OBJECTIVE CASE

PRONOMBRES PERSONALES; CASO ACUSATIVO

Nominativo	Caso acusativo	
I	me	me, a mi
You	you	te, le, a usted
He	him	le, a él
She	her	la, a ella
It	it	le, la a ello, lo
We	us	nos, a nosotros
You	you	les, a ustedes
They	them	les, a ellos, a ellas

1. You see me.   Tú me ves.
2. I see you.   Yo te veo.
3. She sees him.   Ella lo ve (a él).
4. He sees her.   El la ve (a ella).
5. You see it.   Lo ves (animal o cosa).
6. They see us.   Ellos nos ven.
7. We see you.   Nosotros los vemos (a ustedes).
8. You see them.   Tú los ves (a ellos).

EJERCICIO 18	CAMBIA LA PARTE SUBRAYADA POR PRONOMBRES PERSONALES DEL CASO ACUSATIVO: YOU, HIM, HER, IT, US, THEM

E.   I see <u>John</u> on the bus every morning.

I see him on the bus every morning.

1.   I often go to the movies with <u>Suzan.</u>

_____

2.   I like <u>Mary and Kathy</u> very much.

_____

3.   He never speaks to <u>Linda and me.</u>

_____

4.   We also like <u>Helen and Lisa</u> very much.

_____

5.   She writes many letters to <u>her sister.</u>

_____

6.   I sit near <u>William and his brother.</u>

_____

7.   We see <u>Helen</u> in the cafeteria every day.

_____

8.   I understand <u>my teacher, Mr. Arias,</u> very well.

_____

9.   He gives <u>his son</u> a lot of money.

_____

10. She always speaks to <u>her daughter</u> in English.

   _____

11. He sends <u>his sister</u> many presents.

   _____

12. Mark writes many letters to <u>his sister.</u>

   _____

13. I sit near <u>Mary and Helen</u> in the classroom.

   _____

14. Kathy sits near <u>Henry and George.</u>

   _____

15. We write many letters to <u>our parents.</u>

   _____

16. She sees <u>you and Benny</u> on the bus every morning.

   _____

17. I often see <u>those boys</u> in the cafeteria.

   _____

18. I know <u>both Paul and his brother</u> very well.

   _____

19. They usually go to the movies with <u>their parents.</u>

   _____

20. She wants to go to the party with <u>Betty and me.</u>

   _____

LESSON 13

♦ Imperative Form

IMPERATIVE FORM

FORMA IMPERATIVA

La proposición imperativa es una oración en que se hace un mandamiento, una exhortación, o se da una orden. En este caso no es necesario usar la partícula **TO** que acompaña a los verbos en el infinitivo. Hay solamente una forma para el singular y plural y el sujeto **YOU** se entiende pero no se expresa.

Affirmative form

1. Stand up.
2. Please sit down.
3. Open the door, please.
4. Open the window.
5. Come here, please.

Forma afirmativa

Párese.
Siéntese por favor.
Abra la puerta por favor.
Abra la ventana.
Venga acá por favor.

Negative form

1. Don't stand up
2. Don't sit down, please.
3. Don't open the door, please.
4. Don't open the window, please.
5. Please don't go.

Forma negativa

No se pare.
No se siente por favor.
No abra la puerta por favor.
No abra la ventana por favor.
Por favor no se vaya.

EJERCICIO 19   CAMBIA ESTAS ORACIONES IMPERATIVAS A LA FORMA NEGATIVA

E.   Write your exercises in pencil.

<u>Don't write your exercises in pencil.</u>

1.   Come back at two o'clock.

_____

2.   Sit in that chair.

_____

3.   Open the window.

_____

4.   Close the door.

_____

5.   Stand up.

_____

6.   Please go.

_____

7.   Ask Mr. Smith to come in.

_____

8.   Take the next bus.

_____

9.   Wait on that corner.

_____

10.   Put your books there on that desk.

_____

11. Hang your coat on that chair.

     _____

12. Study the next lesson.

     _____

13. Write all the exercises in this lesson.

     _____

14. Help Frank with his lesson.

     _____

15. Speak English in this class.

     _____

16. Give this to Mr. Brown.

     _____

17. Sit in the sun.

     _____

18. Drive fast.

     _____

19. Tell Mary to wait for us.

     _____

20. Put these chairs in the next room.

     _____

LESSON 14

♦ Present Progressive

PRESENT PROGRESSIVE

PRESENTE PROGRESIVO

El presente progresivo (o gerundio) se forma con el presente del verbo **TO BE** (ser, estar) y agregando **ING** (ando, endo, iendo) al verbo que le sigue.

1.	I am working now.	Estoy trabajando ahora.
2.	You are dancing very well.	Estás bailando muy bién.
3.	He is writing a letter.	El está escribiendo una carta.
4.	She is coming home.	Ella viene para la casa.
5.	It is drinking milk.	Está bebiendo leche.
6.	We are learning English.	Estamos aprendiendo inglés.
7.	You are eating lunch.	Ustedes están comiéndose el almuerzo.
8.	They are dancing Merengue.	Ellos está bailando Merengue.
9.	She is pushing the door.	Ella está empujando la puerta.
10.	He is pulling the door.	El está halando la puerta.

EJERCICIO 20   COMPLETA CON EL PRESENTE PROGRESIVO

E.   (work) I_____am working_____ now.

1.   (dance) You _____ very well.

2.   (write) He _____ a letter.

3.   (come) She _____ home.

4.   (drink) It _____ milk.

5.   (learn) We _____ English.

6.   (eat) You _____ lunch.

7.   (dance) They _____ Merengue.

8.   (push) She _____ the door.

9.   (pull) He _____ the car.

10.   (prepare) John _____ his homework now.

11.   (wait) She _____ for me on the corner now.

12.   (begin) Look! It _____ to rain.

13.   (take) They _____ a walk.

14.   (make) We _____ good progress in our courses.

15.   (ring) The telephone _____ now.

16.   (study) We _____ the exercise on page 75 now.

17.   (leave) The plane _____ at this moment.

18.   (look) Kathy _____ for her English book.

19.   (knock) Listen! Someone _____ at the door.

20.   (read) My father _____ the newspaper now.

LESSON 15

- ◆ To Be
- ◆ Past Tense

VERB TO BE; PAST TENSE

VERBO SER, ESTAR; TIEMPO PASADO

I was	Yo era, estaba
You were	Tú eras, estabas
He was	El era, estaba
She was	Ella era, estaba
It was	Era, estaba
We were	Nosotros éramos, estábamos
You were	Ustedes eran, estaban
They were	Ellos, eran, estaban

1. What were you?	¿Qué eras tú?
2. I was a good student.	Yo era un buen estudiante.
3. You were a teacher.	Tú eras un profesor.
4. He was an artist.	El era un artista.
5. She was a nurse.	Ella era una enfermera.
6. Where were you?	¿Dónde estabas?
7. I was in Canada.	Yo estaba en Canadá.
8. We were in the United States.	Nosotros estábamos en los Estados Unidos.
9. You were in Bani.	Ustedes estaban en Baní.
10. They were in Boston.	Ellos estaban en Boston.

EJERCICIO 21   COMPLETA CON WAS O WERE

E.   She _____ was _____ in the classroom this afternoon.

1.   He _____ a good student.

2.   I _____ a good teacher.

3.   Peter _____ in my class.

4.   We _____ good friends.

5.   Helen and Mary _____ in the same class.

6.   The door _____ open.

7.   The windows and the doors _____ closed.

8.   The book _____ on the table.

9.   I _____ very hungry.

10. Linda and John _____ students.

11. Miss Lara_____ our teacher.

12. This _____ an easy exercise.

13. The weather _____ good.

14. We _____ in the United States of America.

15. This lesson _____ easy.

16. You and Frank _____ good friends.

17. Elizabeth and I _____ in Canada.

18. They _____ good students.

19. The doctor _____ at the door.

20. We _____ near the office.

LESSON 16

♦ Past Progressive

PAST PROGRESSIVE

PASADO PROGRESIVO

El pasado progresivo (o gerundio) se forma con el pasado del verbo **TO BE** (ser estar) y agregando **ING** (ando, endo, iendo) al verbo que le sigue.

1.	I was working this morning.	Yo estaba trabajando esta mañana.
2.	You were dancing very well.	Estabas bailando muy bién.
3.	He was writing a letter.	El estaba escribiendo una carta.
4.	She was coming home.	Ella venía para la casa.
5.	It was drinking milk.	Estaba bebiendo leche.
6.	We were learning English.	Estabamos aprendiendo inglés.
7.	You were eating lunch.	Estaban almorzando.
8.	They were dancing Merengue.	Ellos estaban bailando Merengue.
9.	She was pushing the door.	Ella estaba empujando la puerta.
10.	He was pulling the door.	El estaba halando la puerta.

EJERCICIO 22 COMPLETA CON EL PASADO PROGRESIVO

E. (work) I _____<u>was working</u>_____ this morning.

1. (dance) You _____ very well.

2. (write) He _____ a letter.

3. (come) She _____ home.

4. (drink) It _____ milk.

5. (learn) We _____ English and French.

6. (eat) You _____ lunch.

7. (dance) They _____ Rock.

8. (push) She _____ the door.

9. (pull) He _____ his car.

10. (study) Joseph _____ the lesson.

11. (play) The children _____ in the yard.

12. (give) The teacher _____ the book to John.

13. (talk) The women _____ to the teacher.

14. (look) Mr. Sanchez _____ at the newspaper.

15. (count) The cashier _____ the money.

16. (study) They _____ the new words.

17. (hit) The boy _____ the ball.

18. (run) She _____ into the building.

19. (repeat) The students _____ the words carefully.

20. (smile) Kelvin and Mark _____ at the pretty girls.

LESSON 17

- ◆ Past Tense
- ◆ Regular Verbs
- ◆ Irregular Verbs

PAST TENSE OF REGULAR VERBS

TIEMPO PASADO DE VERBOS REGULARES

El tiempo pasado de la mayoría de los verbos en inglés se hace al añadir **ED** a la forma infinitiva del verbo. Todos los verbos que cambian al pasado agregándose **ED** se llaman verbos regulares. El verbo en pasado se usa igual con todos los pronombres. Vea la CUARTA PARTE que trata sobre los verbos regulares e irregulares.

To work	**Trabajar**
I worked	Yo trabajé, trabajaba
You worked	Tú trabajaste, trabajabas
He worked	El trabajó, trabajaba
She worked	Ella trabajó, trabajaba
It worked	Trabajó, trabajaba, funcionó, funcionaba
We worked	Nosotros trabajamos, trabajábamos
You worked	Ustedes trabajaron, trabajaban
They worked	Ellos trabajaron, trabajaban

Si los verbos regulares terminan en **E**, solo se agrega **D**. Si terminan en **Y**, seguida de una consonante, se cambia la **Y** por **I** y se agrega **ED**, pero si los verbos regulares terminan en **Y**, seguida por una vocal, solamente se agrega **ED**.

Dance	Bailar
Danced	Bailé, Bailaste…
Study	Estudiar
Studied	Estudié, Estudiaste…
Play	Jugar
Played	Jugué, Jugaste…

PAST TENSE OF IRREGULAR VERBS

TIEMPO PASADO DE VERBOS IRREGULARES

Muchos verbos comunes en inglés tienen un tiempo pasado de forma especial. El tiempo pasado de estos verbos irregulares debe ser memorizado. Al igual que los verbos regulares estos verbos se conjugan igual en cada pronombre y se llaman verbos irregulares.

To eat	**Comer**
Ate	Comió, comía
I ate	Yo comí, comía
You ate	Tú comiste, comías
He ate	El comió, comía
She ate	Ella comió, comía
It ate	Comió, comía
We ate	Nosotros comimos, comíamos
You ate	Ustedes comieron, comían
They ate	Ellos comieron, comían

EJERCICIO 23	COMPLETA CON EL PASADO DE LOS VERBOS.

E. (study) John _____studied_____ French last year.

1. (live) They _____ in New York for one year.

2. (walk) Mr. Smith _____ in the park last Sunday.

3. (watch) We _____ a baseball game on television.

4. (smoke) I _____ two cigars yesterday.

5. (wash) Mrs. Ramirez _____ the clothes last Monday.

6. (like) Bob _____ the movie last night.

7. (stop) The car _____ in the middle of Duarte street.

8. (listen) We _____ to the radio last night.

9. (rain) It _____ very hard the night before last.

10. (wait) I _____ for them on the corner.

11. (feel) She _____ fine.

12. (drink) Christopher _____ a lot of milk.

13. (wear) She _____ very pretty clothes.

14. (read) We _____ many magazines.

15. (leave) Tom _____ the office at five o'clock.

16. (ride) He _____ to work with Bill.

17. (buy) Kathy _____ groceries at that store.

18. (see) I _____ Betty in that room.

19. (teach) Mr. Brown _____ history and English.

20. (hear) I _____ an airplane.

LESSON 18

- ◆ Auxiliary Verbs
  - ◆ Did
  - ◆ Can
  - ◆ Could
  - ◆ May
  - ◆ Must
  - ◆ Should
  - ◆ Would
- ◆ Question Form
- ◆ Negative Form

AUXILIARY DID

AUXILIAR DID

El auxiliar **DID** se usa para preguntar en el tiempo pasado. **DID** es el pasado de **DO**, y cuando se usa para preguntar no se traduce, ya que el pasado recae en el verbo principal.

1. Did you eat?	¿Comiste?
2. Did he come?	¿Vino él?
3. Did she do her homework?	¿Ella hizo la tarea?
4. Did we go to Canada?	¿Fuimos a Canada?
5. Did you go to the hospital?	¿Fuiste al hospital?
6. Did they paint their house?	¿Pintaron ellos su casa?
7. What did you do?	¿Qué hiciste?
8. Did you work yesterday?	¿Trabajaste ayer?

Se usa **DID NOT** o **DIDN'T** para la forma negativa en el tiempo pasado y, al igual que en las preguntas, los verbos se quedan en el infinitivo o forma original.

1. I didn't eat rice.	Yo no comí arroz.
2. You didn't go to school.	Tú no fuiste a la escuela.
3. He didn't drive a bus.	El no manejó un autobús.
4. She didn't drink beer.	Ella no tomó cerveza.
5. It didn't rain yesterday.	No llovió ayer.
6. We didn't close the door.	No cerramos la puerta.
7. You didn't listen to me.	Ustedes no me escucharon.
8. They didn't wait for us.	Ellos no nos esperaron.

EJERCICIO 24

CAMBIA A LA FORMA INTERROGATIVA. USA DID

E.   You went to Canada.

<u>Did you go to Canada?</u>

1.   He sold the car.

_____

2.   John bought a new pair of shoes.

_____

3.   He spoke to the girl after class.

_____

4.   She said something interesting.

_____

5.   They went to the baseball game.

_____

6.   She brought a friend to school.

_____

7.   Mr. Lopez wore a new shirt.

_____

8.   The students came at eight o'clock.

_____

9.   He made a mistake on the test.

_____

10. The boys held the box carefully.

_____

11. Frank wrote the answer on the paper.

_____

12. Tommy and Peter ate some sandwiches.

_____

13. You drank too much coffee last night.

_____

14. They felt very bad this morning.

_____

15. The train left at 5:30 P.M.

_____

16. Mary chose a pretty skirt.

_____

17. Mr. Arias taught English last year.

_____

18. Benny put the money in his wallet.

_____

19. We found the purse on the floor.

_____

20. They heard that radio program.

_____

AUXILIARY CAN

AUXILIAR CAN (PODER)

1.	I can speak English.	Yo puedo hablar Inglés.
2.	You can walk to school.	Tú puedes caminar hacia la escuela.
3.	He can write a letter.	El puede escribir una carta.
4.	She can eat potatoes.	Ella puede comer papas.
5.	It can run fast.	Puede correr rápidamente.
6.	We can speak Spanish.	Nosotros podemos hablar español.
7.	You can come tonight.	Ustedes pueden venir esta noche.
8.	They can clean the car.	Ellos pueden limpiar el carro.
9.	She can type a letter.	Ella puede escribir a máquina una carta.
10.	He can drive a car.	El puede manejar un carro.

AUXILARY COULD

AUXILIAR COULD (PUDO, PODRIA)

Could es el pasado de Can (poder).

1.	I could speak English.	Yo pude (podría) hablar Inglés.
2.	You could walk to school.	Tú pudiste (podrías) caminar hacia la escuela.
3.	He could write a letter.	El pudo (podría) escribir una carta.
4.	She could eat potatoes.	Ella pudo (podría) comer papas.
5.	It could run fast.	Pudo (podría) correr rápidamente.
6.	We could speak Spanish.	Pudimos (podríamos) hablar Español.
7.	You could come tonight.	Ustedes pudieron (podrían) venir esta noche.
8.	They could clean the car.	Ellos pudieron (podrían) limpiar el carro.
9.	She could type a letter.	Ella pudo (podría) escribir a máquina una carta.
10.	He could drive a car.	El pudo (podría) manejar un carro.

AUXILIARY MAY

AUXLILIAR MAY (PODER)

1.	May I come in?	¿Puedo entrar?
2.	You may go now.	Te puedes ir ahora.
3.	He may speak Spanish here.	El puede hablar español aquí.
4.	She may clean the house.	Ella puede limpiar la casa.
5.	It may be true.	Puede ser verdad.
6.	We may write letters to them.	Podemos escribir cartas a ellos.
7.	You may drink this medicine.	Ustedes pueden tomar esta medicina.
8.	They may taste the cookies.	Ellos pueden probar las galletitas.
9.	He may do his homework now.	El puede hacer su tarea ahora.
10.	She may buy the red umbrella.	Ella puede comprar la sombrilla roja.

AUXILIARY MUST

AUXILIAR MUST (DEBER)

1.	I must eat every day.	Debo comer cada día.
2.	You must take a bath daily	Debes bañarte diariamente.
3.	He must see a doctor.	El debe ver un doctor.
4.	She must drink a lot of water.	Ella debe beber mucha agua.
5.	It must be late.	Debe ser tarde.
6.	We must get married.	Debemos casarnos.
7.	You must do exercises.	Ustedes deben hacer ejercicios.
8.	They must swim in the afternoon.	Ellos deben nadar en la tarde.
9.	He must write a book.	El debe escribir un libro.
10.	She must visit her parents.	Ella debe visitar a sus padres.

AUXILIARY SHOULD

AUXILIAR SHOULD (DEBERIA)

1.	I should go to school every day.	Debería ir a la escuela cada día.
2.	You should brush your teeth.	Deberías cepillarte los dientes.
3.	He should tell her the truth.	El debería decirle (a ella) la verdad.
4.	She should come earlier.	Ella debería venir más temprano.
5.	It should be black.	Debería ser negro.
6.	We should go home now.	Deberíamos irnos a la casa ahora.
7.	You should work in the afternoon.	Ustedes deberían trabajar en la tarde.
8.	They should drink a lot of juice.	Ellos deberían beber mucho jugo.

AUXILIARY WOULD

AUXILIAR WOULD

Este auxiliar se usa para dar el equivalente **IA** en español.

1.	I would like to speak English.	Me gustaría hablar Inglés.
2.	You would do it in one hour.	Usted lo haría en una hora.
3.	He would come to class.	El vendría a la clase.
4.	She would wash the dishes.	Ella lavaría los platos.
5.	We would like to write letters.	Nos gustaría escribir cartas.
6.	You would clean the windows.	Ustedes limpiarían las ventanas.
7.	They would wash the doors.	Ellos lavarían las puertas.

AUXILIARY VERBS; QUESTION FORM

VERBOS AUXILIARES, FORMA INTERROGATIVA

1.	Can you speak English?	¿Puedes hablar Inglés?
2.	Could you speak English?	¿Podrías hablar Inglés?
3.	Did you read this book?	¿Leíste este libro?
4.	May I use this pen?	¿Puedo usar este lapicero?
5.	Should you go to the hospital?	¿Deberías ir al hospital?
6.	Can she carry this chair?	¿Puede ella levantar esta silla?
7.	Could she carry this chair?	¿Podría ella cargar esta silla?
8.	Would you like to paint the house?	¿Te gustaría pintar la casa?
9.	May we smoke here?	¿Podemos fumar aquí?
10.	Should I stay in this room?	¿Debería quedarme en este cuarto?

EJERCICIO 25   CAMBIA A LA FORMA INTERROGATIVA

E.   She can speak French well.

   Can she speak French well?

1.   He should wait on that corner.

   _____

2.   I may smoke here.

   _____

3.   He must go out of town.

   _____

4.   You would like to go to the movies.

   _____

5.   I could meet you at two o'clock.

   _____

6.   She can go with us tonight.

   _____

7.   We should tell Helen about it.

   _____

8.   I may wait in Mary's office.

   _____

9.   They must explain it to him.

   _____

10. You could wait in his office.

   _____

11. We may sit here.

_____

12. You would like to drink coffee.

_____

13. He should stay at home.

_____

14. She can meet us after dinner.

_____

15. You must write him a letter.

_____

16. I may wait here.

_____

17. She should sit near the window.

_____

18. John can play the violin well.

_____

19. You would like to swim today.

_____

20. She must go tomorrow.

_____

AUXILIARY VERBS; NEGATIVE FORM

VERBOS AUXILIARES; FORMA NEGATIVA

1. I can not speak French.   No puedo hablar francés.
2. You could not understand what she said.   No pudiste entender lo que ella dijo.
3. He must not go to Canada this year.   El no debe ir a Canada este año.
4. I may not go in now.   No puedo entrar ahora.
5. You should not call the police.   No deberías llamar la policía.
6. We must not speak Spanish in this class.   No debemos hablar español en esta clase.
7. She would not like to live in this country.   A ella no le gustaría vivir en este país.
8. They can not carry that couch.   Ellos no pueden cargar ese mueble.
9. We did not study French or German.   Nosotros no estudiamos francés o alemán.
10. He could not type all the letters.   El no pudo escribir a máquina todas las cartas.

Las contracciones con los auxiliares son las siguientes:

Can not	Can't
Could not	Couldn't
Do not	Don't
Does not	Doesn't
Did not	Didn't
Must not	Mustn't
Should not	Shouldn't
Will not	Won't
Would not	Wouldn't

EJERCICIO 26   CAMBIA A LA FORMA NEGATIVA

E.   Frank can speak English very well.

Frank can not speak English very well.

1.   He should speak Spanish in the classroom.

_____

2.   You may smoke here.

_____

3.   She must see him.

_____

4.   I can call her later.

_____

5.   We would like to go on foot.

_____

6.   They could see the movie.

_____

7.   You should tell her about it.

_____

8.   We may open the window.

_____

9.   I must tell John about the problem.

_____

10. She can play the piano very well.

_____

11.   I would like to wash the car.

   _____

12.   We could do all of these exercises.

   _____

13.   They should be back before noon.

   _____

14.   Janet may go to the party with us.

   _____

15.   We must do that again.

   _____

16.   They can meet us later.

   _____

17.   She would like to clean the house.

   _____

18.   I could understand her well.

   _____

19.   He should sit near the window.

   _____

20.   You may come in now.

   _____

LESSON 19

- ♦ Future Tense
  - ♦ Will
  - ♦ Going To

FUTURE TENSE USING WILL AND GOING TO

TIEMPO FUTURO USANDO WILL Y GOING TO.

Para hacer el tiempo futuro en Inglés se puede usar el auxiliar **WILL** y también **GOING TO**.

1. I will study English in Canada.
   I am going to study English in Canada.   Estudiaré inglés en Canada.

2. You will read this book.
   You are going to read this book.   Leerás este libro.

3. He will translate the sentences.
   He is going to translate the sentences.   El traducirá las oraciones.

4. She will come at five o'clock.
   She is going to come at five o'clock.   Ella vendrá a las cinco en punto.

5. It will be easy for me.
   It is going to be easy for me.   Sera fácil para mi.

6. We will eat lunch here
   We are going to eat lunch here.   Almorzaremos aquí.

7. You will speak on the phone
   You are going to speak on the phone.   Ustedes hablarán por teléfono.

8. They will buy this book
   They are going to buy this book.   Ellos comprarán este libro.

EJERCICIO 27

CAMBIA AL FUTURO.
USA WILL Y GOING TO

E. I read this book.

I will read this book.

I am going to read this book.

1. He studies in this class.

2. She works in this office.

3. You speak English very well.

4. I come to the lesson on time.

5. They walk to their work.

6. He brings his friends to the class.

7.   She opens the door for us.

_____

_____

8.   They study very much.

_____

_____

9.   She brings all her books to the lesson.

_____

_____

10.   He plays the violin very well.

_____

_____

11.   We carry all the small packages.

_____

_____

12.   She speaks to us in English.

_____

_____

13.   He writes a letter to his mother every day.

_____

_____

14.   I bring you many presents.

_____

_____

15. She arrives to the classroom on time.

_____

_____

16. He works from nine to five.

_____

_____

17. They eat all their meals in the cafeteria.

_____

_____

18. The train leaves at eight o'clock.

_____

_____

19. You like that teacher very much.

_____

_____

20. She teaches us English and Mathematics.

_____

_____

LESSON 20

- ◆ Information Questions
  - ◆ What
  - ◆ Where
  - ◆ When
  - ◆ How
  - ◆ Why

INFORMATION QUESTIONS USING WHAT

PREGUNTAS INFORMATIVAS USANDO WHAT (QUE)

1. What's your name?
    My name is Frank.

    ¿Cuál es tu nombre?
    Mi nombre es Frank.

2. What's this?
    That's a book.

    ¿Qué es esto?
    Eso es un libro.

3. What's your nationality?
    I am Dominican.

    ¿Cuál es tu nacionalidad?
    Soy Dominicano.

4. What do you do?
    I'm a teacher.

    ¿Qué haces?
    Soy profesor.

5. What time is it?
    It's two o'clock

    ¿Qué hora es?
    Son las dos en punto.

6. What can you do?
    I can speak English.

    ¿Qué puedes hacer?
    Puedo hablar inglés.

7. What must you do?
    I must go to the hospital.

    ¿Qué debes hacer?
    Debo ir al hospital.

8. What should you drink?
    I should drink lemonade.

    ¿Qué deberías beber?
    Debería beber limonada.

9. What did you eat?
    I ate some cookies.

    ¿Qué comiste?
    Me comí algunas galletas.

10. What did you buy?
    I bought some clothes.

    ¿Que compraste?
    Compré algunas ropas.

INFORMATION QUESTIONS USING WHERE

PREGUNTAS INFORMATIVAS USANDO WHERE (DONDE)

1. Where were you?
   I was in Bani.

   ¿Dónde estabas?
   Yo estaba en Baní

2. Where did you learn English?
   I learned English at home.

   ¿Dónde aprendiste inglés?
   Aprendí inglés en la casa.

3. Where were you studying?
   I was studying at the university.

   ¿Dónde estabas estudiando?
   Yo estaba estudiando en la universidad.

4. Where is your father?
   He is in the countryside.

   ¿Dónde esta tu padre?
   El está en el campo.

5. Where do you work?
   I work at school.

   ¿Dónde trabajas?
   Trabajo en la escuela.

6. Where did you buy this book?
   I bought it at the bookstore.

   ¿Dónde compraste este libro?
   Lo compré en la librería.

7. Where was she cooking?
   She was cooking in the kitchen.

   ¿Dónde estaba ella cocinando?
   Ella estaba cocinando en la cocina.

8. Where does he come from?
   He comes from Canada.

   ¿De dónde viene él?
   El viene de Canadá.

9. Where can I eat lunch?
   You can eat lunch at the restaurant.

   ¿Dónde puedo almorzar?
   Tu puedes almorzar en el restaurante.

10. Where must they go?
    They must go to the doctor.

    ¿A dónde deben ir?
    Ellos deben ir al doctor.

INFORMATION QUESTIONS USING WHEN

PREGUNTAS INFORMATIVAS USANDO WHEN (CUANDO)

1. When did you come? — ¿Cuándo viniste?
   I came yesterday. — Vine ayer.

2. When must you do it? — ¿Cuándo debes hacerlo?
   I must do it today. — Debo hacerlo hoy.

3. When should you go? — ¿Cuándo deberias ir?
   I should go next week. — Debería ir la próxima semana.

4. When is the party? — ¿Cuándo es la fiesta?
   The party will be next month. — La fiesta será el próximo mes.

5. When are you going to the capital? — ¿Cuando irás a la capital?
   I'm going tomorrow. — Iré mañana.

6. When did you buy this radio? — ¿Cuándo compraste este radio?
   I bought it two months ago. — Lo compré hace dos meses.

7. When could you do this job? — ¿Cuándo podrías hacer este trabajo?
   I could do it in two weeks. — Lo haría en dos semanas.

8. When must you come? — ¿Cuándo debes venir?
   I must come in March. — Debo venir en marzo.

9. When is your sister going to come from Canada? — ¿Cuándo vendrá tu hermana de Canadá?
   She is going to come in September. — Ella vendrá en septiembre.

10. When did you write this book? — ¿Cuándo escribiste este libro?
    I wrote it last year. — Lo escribí el año pasado.

INFORMATION QUESTIONS USING HOW

PREGUNTAS INFORMATIVAS USANDO HOW (COMO)

1. How are you?
   Very well, thank you.
   ¿Cómo estas?
   Muy bién, gracias.
2. How will you go?
   I will go by plane.
   ¿Cómo te irás?
   Me iré por avión.
3. How should you come?
   I should come on foot.
   ¿Cómo deberías venir?
   Debería venir a pie.
4. How would you like to write?
   I would like to write in English.
   ¿Cómo te gustaría escribir?
   Me gustaría escribir en inglés.
5. How did she learn Spanish?
   She learned at the university.
   ¿Cómo aprendió ella Español?
   Ella aprendió en la universidad.
6. How do you turn on this radio?
   I turn it on by pushing this button.
   ¿Cómo prendes este radio?
   Lo prendo presionando este botón.
7. How will you go back home?
   I will go back by plane.
   ¿Cómo te irás de regreso a casa?
   Regresaré por avión.
8. How did you arrive?
   I arrived by bus.
   ¿Cómo llegaste?
   Llegué por autobús.
9. How will you travel next year?
   I will travel by train.
   ¿Cómo viajarás el próximo año?
   Viajaré por tren.
10. How did you learn English?
    I learned it by mail.
    ¿Cómo aprendiste inglés?
    Lo aprendí por correspondencia.

INFORMATION QUESTIONS USING WHY

PREGUNTAS INFORMATIVAS USANDO WHY (POR QUE)

1. Why do you study English?   ¿Por qué estudias Inglés?
   Because I like to travel.   Porque me gusta viajar.

2. Why does he live in Ocoa?   ¿Por qué vive él en Ocoa?
   Because it is a beautiful town.   Porque es un pueblo bonito.

3. Why must she go to the hospital?   ¿Por qué debe ella ir al hospital?
   Because she's sick.   Porque ella está enferma.

4. Why should they come tomorrow?   ¿Por qué deberían venir mañana?
   Because they have to explain the homework.   Porque tienen que explicar las tarea.

5. Why are you doing exercises?   ¿Por qué estás haciendo ejercicios?
   Because I would like to be strong.   Porque me gustaría ser fuerte.

6. Why did she come today?   ¿Por qué ella vino hoy?
   Because she had some problems with the car.   Porque tuvo algunos problemas con el carro.

7. Why do you like to speak English?   ¿Por qué te gusta hablar Inglés?
   Because it is an important language.   Porque es un idioma importante.

8. Why are you drinking water?   ¿Por qué estás tomando agua?
   Because I am thirsty.   Porque tengo sed.

9. Why did you buy this car?   ¿Por qué compraste este carro?
   Because I need it.   Porque lo necesito.

10. Why didn't you come to class yesterday?   ¿Por qué no viniste a clase ayer?
    Because I couldn't find my book.   Porque no pude encontrar mi libro.

EJERCICIO 28

COMPLETA CON
WHAT, WHERE, HOW, WHY, WHEN

E. _____What_____ color is that book?

It's blue.

1. _____ is your name?

My name is Mary.

2. _____ do you live?

I live in Pennsylvania.

3. _____ did you come?

I came in September.

4. _____ are you?

I'm fine, thanks.

5. _____ do you study English?

Because it's very important for me.

6. _____ is that?

It's a pen.

7. _____ did you learn English?

I learned English in Canada.

8. _____ must you do it?

I must do it tomorrow.

9. _____ will you go to the capital?

I will go there by bus.

10. _____ does he live in New York?

Because he has relatives there.

11. _____ is your nationality?

    I'm Dominican.

12. _____ is your father?

    He's at home.

13. _____ should you go?

    I should go now.

14. _____ do you turn on this radio?

    By pushing this button.

15. _____ are you doing exercises?

    Because I want to lose weight.

16. _____ time is it?

    It's five o'clock.

17. _____ did you buy this book?

    I bought it in Miami.

18. _____ could you do this job?

    I could do it this afternoon.

19. _____ will you go back home?

    I will go back by plane.

20. _____ didn't you come to class yesterday?

    Because I was sick.

LESSON 21

- ◆ Information Questions
  - ◆ How Many
  - ◆ How Much

INFORMATION QUESTIONS USING HOW MANY

PREGUNTAS INFORMATIVAS USANDO HOW MANY (CUANTOS, CUANTAS)

1. How many brothers do you have?

   ¿Cuántos hermanos tú tienes?

   I have four brothers.

   Tengo cuatro hermanos.

2. How many sisters do you have?

   ¿Cuántas hermanas tienes?

   I have two sisters.

   Tengo dos hermanas.

3. How many pencils did you buy?

   ¿Cuantos lápices compraste?

   I bought three pencils.

   Compré tres lápices.

4. How many books can you take?

   ¿Cuántos libros puedes llevar?

   I can take ten books.

   Puedo llevar diez libros.

5. How many houses did you paint?

   ¿Cuántas casas pintaste?

   I painted five houses.

   Pinté cinco casas.

6. How many chairs are there in this room?

   ¿Cuántas sillas hay en este cuarto?

   There are six chairs in this room.

   Hay seis sillas en este cuarto.

7. How many pictures are there on the wall?

   ¿Cuantos cuadros hay en la pared?

   There are seven pictures on the wall.

   Hay siete cuadros en la pared.

8. How many pens do you need?

   ¿Cuantos lapiceros necesitas?

   I need ten pens.

   Necesito diez lapiceros.

9. How many children would you like to have?

   ¿Cuántos niños te gustaría tener?

   I would like to have four children

   Me gustaría tener cuatro niños.

10. How many books did you buy yesterday?

    ¿Cuántos libros compraste ayer?

    I bought eight books yesterday.

    Compré ocho libros ayer.

INFORMATION QUESTIONS USING HOW MUCH

PREGUNTAS INFORMATIVAS USANDO HOW MUCH (CUANTO, QUE CANTIDAD)

1. How much money do you need?

   ¿Qué cantidad de dinero necesitas?

   I need a lot of money.

   Necesito mucho dinero.

2. How much milk do you drink a day?

   ¿Qué cantidad de leche tomas al día?

   I drink three glasses of milk.

   Me tomo tres vasos de leche.

3. How much water do you need?

   ¿Qué cantidad de agua necesitas?

   I need a gallon.

   Necesito un galón.

4. How much time do you take to arrive here?

   ¿Cuánto tiempo te tomas para llegar aquí.

   I take fifteen minutes to arrive here.

   Me tomo quince minutos para llegar aquí

5. How much meat do you want?

   ¿Qué cantidad de carne quieres?

   I want a pound of meat.

   Quiero una libra de carne.

6. How much water can you drink a day?

   ¿Qué cantidad de agua puedes tomarte al día?

   I can drink six glasses of water a day.

   Me puedo tomar seis vasos de agua al dia.

7. How much ham do you need?

   ¿Qué cantidad de jamón necesitas?

   I need two pieces of ham.

   Necesito dos pedazos de jamón.

8. How much juice would you like to drink?

   ¿Qué cantidad de jugo te gustaría tomar?

   I would like to drink two glasses of juice.

   Me gustaría tomarme dos vasos de jugo.

9. How much are those shoes?

   ¿Cuánto cuestan esos zapatos?

   Those shoes are one hundred dollars.

   Esos zapatos cuestan cien dólares.

10. How much money do you have?

    ¿Qué cantidad de dinero tienes?

    I have ten dollars.

    Tengo diez dólares.

EJERCICIO 29	COMPLETA CON HOW MUCH O HOW MANY

E. _____How many_____ pens do you have?

1. _____ lemon do you want in your tea?

2. _____ bottles of milk do you need?

3. _____ questions are there in this exercise?

4 _____ candy did you eat yesterday?

5 _____ cups of coffee did you order?

6 _____ coffee did the men order?

7 _____ oil does this car use?

8. _____ workmen are there in that factory?

9 _____ brothers do you have?

10. _____ money do you need?

11. _____ pencils did you buy?

12 _____ milk do you drink a day?

13. _____ books can you take in your hands?

14. _____ water do you need?

15. _____ houses did you paint?

16. _____ time do you take to arrive here?

17. _____ chairs are there in this room?

18. _____ meat do you want?

19. _____ pictures are there on the wall?

20. _____ juice would you like to drink?

LESSON 22

- ◆ Adjectives
- ◆ Adverbs
- ◆ Comparative Degree
- ◆ Superlative Degree

ADJECTIVES—ADVERBS

ADJETIVOS—ADVERBIOS

Un adjetivo es una palabra que describe un nombre. Un adverbio es una palabra que generalmente modifica o describe un verbo. Indica como hacemos algo. Los adverbios generalmente terminan en – **ly**.

1. I am a beautiful girl.
   I play the piano beautifully.

   Yo soy una muchacha hermosa.
   Yo toco el piano hermosamente.

2. You are a clever boy.
   You did the work cleverly.

   Tú eres un muchacho inteligente.
   Hiciste el trabajo inteligentemente.

3. He is a careful teacher.
   He prepares his lessons carefully.

   El es un profesor cuidadoso.
   El prepara sus lecciones cuidadosamente.

4. She has a slow watch.
   She also walks slowly.

   Ella tiene un reloj lento.
   Ella también camina lentamente.

5. This is an easy exercise.
   We can do it easily.

   Este es un ejercicio facil.
   Podemos hacerlo fácilmente.

6. They are serious students.
   They study English seriously.

   Ellos son estudiantes serios.
   Ellos estudian inglés seriamente.

EJERCICIO 30 — COMPLETA CON LA FORMA CORRECTA DE ADJETIVO O ADVERBIO

E.   (beautiful) Mary plays the piano __beautifully__.

1.   (beautiful) She is a _____ girl.

2.   (soft) This apple is _____

3.   (soft) Miss Smith always speaks very_____

4.   (clever) John did the work very_____

5.   (clever) He is a very_____ boy.

6.   (careful) Helen always prepares her lessons_____

7.   (careful) She is an exceptionally_____ student.

8.   (slow) My watch is_____

9.   (slow) The old man walks very_____

10. (quick) He does all his work_____

11. (easy) This is an_____ exercise.

12. (easy) I can do this exercise_____

13. (frequent) I see her very_____ in the cafeteria.

14. (frequent) He is a_____ visitor in our home.

15. (serious) They are both_____ students.

16. (serious) They both study English very_____

17. (careless) John did the work very_____

18. (careless) He is a very_____ workman.

19. (foolish) That was a very_____ thing to say.

20. (foolish) Kathy acted very_____ in that matter.

ADJECTIVES; COMPARATIVE DEGREE

ADJETIVOS; GRADO COMPARATIVO

El grado comparativo de la mayoría de los adjetivos se hace al agregarse—**ER**. Si el adjetivo tiene más de dos sílabas se hace el comparativo con **MORE** (más). La forma comparativa de los adjetivos está generalmente seguida de la palabra **THAN** (que).

1.	I am taller than my sister.	Soy más alto que mi hermana.
2.	You are younger than your brother.	Tú eres más joven que tu hermano.
3.	He is more intelligent than his father.	El es más inteligente que su padre.
4.	She is more beautiful than Mary.	Ella es más hermosa que Mary.
5.	We are busier today than yesterday.	Hoy estamos más ocupados que ayer.
6.	They are more peaceful today than yesterday.	Ellos están hoy más pacíficos que ayer.

EJERCICIO 31

COMPLETA CON EL GRADO COMPARATIVO DE LOS ADJETIVOS

E. (young) Helen is _____ younger _____ than Mary.

1. (sweet) Oranges are_____ than lemons.

2. (warm) The weather today is_____ than it was yesterday.

3. (interesting) This book is_____ than that one.

4. (easy) This exercise is_____ than the last one.

5. (intelligent) Kathy is_____ than her sister.

6. (cold) February is_____ than March.

7. (large) Our classroom is_____ than your classroom.

8. (long) This lesson is_____ than the next one.

9. (busy) You seem to be_____ today than you were yesterday.

10. (wide) Park Avenue is_____ than Fifth Avenue.

11. (short) February is_____ than May.

12. (peaceful) The sea looks_____ today than it looked yesterday.

13. (high) Prices are_____ this year than they were last year.

14. (beautiful) These flowers are_____ than those in your garden.

15. (late) We arrived at the party_____ than they.

16. (soon) We will get there_____ than you.

17. (early) He called_____ than usual.

18. (fast) Paul drives even_____ than his father.

19. (deep) The Mississippi River is much_____ than any Dominican River.

20. (fast) You can run_____ than I.

ADJECTIVES; SUPERLATIVE DEGREE

ADJETIVOS; GRADO SUPERLATIVO

El grado superlativo se forma al agregar **EST** a la mayoría de los adjetivos. Si el adjetivo tiene más de dos sílabas, generalmente se forma el superlativo con **MOST**.

1. I am the tallest boy in my class.

   Soy el muchacho más alto en mi clase.

2. You are the most beautiful girl at this school.

   Tú eres las muchacha más hermosa en esta escuela.

3. He is the most intelligent man in Mexico.

   El es el hombre más inteligente en México.

4. She is the busiest teacher at our school.

   Ella es la profesora más ocupada en nuestra escuela.

5. This is the most difficult exercise.

   Este es el ejercicio más difícil.

6. We are the youngest boys in our class.

   Somos los muchachos más jóvenes en nuestra clase.

7. They are the prettiest girls in our group.

   Ellas son las muchachas más bonitas en nuestro grupo.

EJERCICIO 32
COMPLETA CON EL GRADO SUPERLATIVO DE LOS ADJETIVOS

E.   (young) John is the _____ youngest _____ boy in the class.

1.   (comfortable) This is the_____ chair in the room.

2.   (easy) These exercises are the_____ of all.

3.   (large) The Pacific Ocean is the_____ ocean in the world.

4.   (expensive) We visited the_____ nightclub in town.

5.   (young) He is the_____ boy in my family.

6.   (cold) December is the_____ month of the year in the
     United States of America.

7.   (intelligent) She is the_____ student in our class.

8.   (large) That store is the_____ one in town.

9.   (tall) Mr. Ramirez is the_____ teacher in my school.

10. (pretty) Margaret is the_____ girl in their group.

11. (busy) Mrs. Silver is the_____ teacher in our school.

12. (wide) Park Avenue is the_____ street in New York City.

13. (difficult) This exercise is the_____ one in the whole book.

14. (tall) Lucy is the_____ girl in our class.

15. (beautiful) She is the_____ girl in this university.

16. (large) New York City is the_____ city in the United States.

17. (intelligent) Suzan is the_____ woman in my class.

18. (long) The Mississippi River is the_____ river in the United States.

19. (easy) This is not the_____ exercise in this book.

20. (fast) That car is the_____ one in the city.

LESSON 23

- ◆ Some
- ◆ Any

SOME, ANY

ALGUNOS, NINGUNOS

Se usa **SOME** en oraciones afirmativas y **ANY** en oraciones negativas e interrogativas.

1.	I saw some cars in the street.	Ví algunos carros en la calle.
2.	You didn't see any.	No viste ninguno.
3.	He has some new magazines.	El tiene algunas revistas nuevas.
4.	She doesn't have any brothers.	Ella no tiene ningún hermano.
5.	There aren't any books on the table.	No hay ningún libro en la mesa.
6.	We don't have any money.	Nosotros no tenemos nada de dinero.
7.	They gave him some money.	Ellos le dieron un poco de dinero.
8.	There are some pictures on the wall.	Hay algunas fotos en la pared.
9.	Do you have any new books?	¿Tienes algunos libros nuevos?
10.	Did you buy any tomatoes?	¿Compraste algunos tomates?

EJERCICIO 33   COMPLETA CON SOME O ANY

E. We don't have _____ any _____ money.

1. They don't want_____ coffee.

2. The boys want_____ dessert now.

3. William is eating_____ ice cream now.

4. He doesn't want_____ sugar in the coffee.

5. There aren't_____ chairs in that room.

6. There are_____ paintings on the wall.

7. I don't want_____ dessert after dinner.

8. She doesn't know_____ words in Russian.

9. He's putting_____ salt and pepper on the table.

10. I don't have_____ time right now.

11. Do you know_____ new songs?

12. He needs_____ money.

13. She is eating_____ candy.

14. They don't have_____ money now.

15. There isn't_____ milk on the table.

16. Are there_____ sandwiches here?

17. Mr. Green knows_____ Spanish.

18. The men want_____ coffee now.

19. He's putting_____ sugar in the coffee.

20. There aren't_____ students in this room.

LESSON 24

♦ Very
♦ Too

VERY, TOO

MUY, DEMASIADO

Algunas veces se confunde el uso de **VERY** (muy) y de **TOO** (demasiado). **VERY** significa mucho, muy, en gran cantidad; mientras que **TOO** siempre sugiere algo en exceso, más de lo que necesitamos o podamos usar.

1.	The blue pen is very big.	El lapicero azul es muy grande.
2.	The blue pen is too big.	El lapicero azul es demasiado grande.
3.	This ring is very small.	Este anillo es muy pequeño.
4.	This ring is too small.	Este anillo es demasiado pequeño.
5.	That magazine is very large.	Esa revista es muy grande.
6.	That magazine is too large.	Esa revista es demasiado grande.
7.	She is very tired.	Ella está muy cansada.
8.	She is too tired.	Ella está demasiado cansada.

EJERCICIO 34   COMPLETA CON TOO O VERY

E.   The red book is _____very_____ big, but it will go into my pocket.

1.   I cannot wear this ring because it is _____small for my finger.

2.   This magazine is_____large, but it will go into my desk.

3.   That other magazine, however, is _____large to go into my desk drawer.

4.   That chair is _____heavy for Linda. She cannot pick it up.

5.   It is a _____heavy chair, but Frank is strong and can easily pick it up.

6.   You are speaking_____fast. I cannot understand you.

7.   Our teacher speaks_____fast, but I always understand him.

8.   This soup is_____hot. I cannot eat it.

9.   The weather in Canada is_____cold in winter, but Mr. Ortiz enjoys it very much.

10. I cannot go out now. It is raining_____hard.

11. The sun was_____hot for the child, and he became sick.

12. It is_____late, but if we hurry we can still catch the bus.

13. Lisa says that she is_____tired to go for a walk with us.

14. The doctor says that Janet is still_____weak to go to work.

15. Benny studies French_____hard and is making good progress.

16. Some of these exercises are_____hard for me. I cannot understand them.

17. This wine is_____sour to drink. It will make me sick.

18. These shoes are_____small for me. They hurt my feet.

19. It is_____cold to go to the beach today. We will all catch cold.

20. It was_____cold, but we all went for a walk in the park.

LESSON 25

◆ Possessive Pronouns

POSSESSIVE PRONOUNS

PRONOMBRES POSESIVOS

I	mine	mío, míos
You	yours	tuyo, tuyos
He	his	suyo, suyos (de él)
She	hers	suyo, suyos (de ella)
We	ours	nuestro, nuestros
You	yours	suyo, suyos (de ustedes)
They	theirs	suyo, suyos (de ellos)

1. This book is mine. — Este libro es mío.
   These books are mine. — Estos libros son míos.
2. That table is yours. — Esa mesa es tuya.
   Those tables are yours. — Esas mesas son tuyas.
3. This pen is his. — Este lapicero es suyo (de él).
   These pens are his. — Estos lapiceros son suyos (de él).
4. That piano is hers. — Ese piano es suyo (de ella).
   Those pianos are hers. — Esos pianos son suyos (de ella).
5. That house is ours. — Esa casa es nuestra.
   Those houses are ours. — Esas casas son nuestras.
6. This car is yours. — Este carro es suyo (de ustedes)
   These cars are yours. — Estos carros son suyos (de ustedes).
7. That pencil is theirs. — Ese lápiz es suyo (de ellos).
   Those pencils are theirs. — Esos lapices son suyos (de ellos).

E. This book is <u>her book.</u>

This book is hers.

1. These pencils are <u>my pencils.</u>

_____

2. This office is <u>his office.</u>

_____

3. These magazines are <u>our magazines.</u>

_____

4. These books are <u>my books.</u>

_____

5. Those pictures on the table are <u>your pictures.</u>

_____

6. These pens are <u>their pens.</u>

_____

7. I think that this notebook is <u>your notebook.</u>

_____

8. This newspaper is <u>my newspaper.</u>

_____

9. This clock is <u>her clock.</u>

_____

10. That hat is <u>his hat.</u>

_____

11. This umbrella is <u>our umbrella.</u>

   _____

12. These seats are <u>their seats.</u>

   _____

13. That pair of shoes is <u>her pair of shoes.</u>

   _____

14. This classroom is <u>my classroom.</u>

   _____

15. That chair is <u>his chair.</u>

   _____

16. These books are <u>our books.</u>

   _____

17. Those calendars over there on the desk are <u>their calendars.</u>

   _____

18. This eraser is <u>your eraser.</u>

   _____

19. That table in this room is <u>my table.</u>

   _____

20. These English books are <u>his English books.</u>

   _____

NOTA: En este caso los PRONOMBRES POSESIVOS se usan para evitar repetición.

LESSON 26

♦ Reflexive Pronouns

REFLEXIVE PRONOUNS

PRONOMBRES REFLEXIVOS

I	myself	Yo mismo
You	yourself	Tú mismo
He	himself	El mismo
She	herself	Ella misma
It	itself	Lo mismo
We	ourselves	Nosotros mismos
You	yourselves	Ustedes mismos
They	themselves	Ellos mismos

1. I shave myself every week.   Me afeito cada semana.
2. You hurt yourself when you fell.   Te heriste cuando te caiste.
3. He enjoyed himself at the party.   El se divirtió en la fiesta.
4. She cut herself with a knife.   Ella se cortó con un cuchillo.
5. The dog hurt itself when it jumped over the fence.   El perro se hirió cuando saltó por encima del cercado.
6. We dressed ourselves in the bathroom.   Nos vestimos en el baño.
7. You burned yourselves on the stove.   Ustedes se quemaron en la estufa.
8. We cut ourselves with this knife.   Nos cortamos con este cuchillo.

EJERCICIO 36

COMPLETA CON PRONOMBRES REFLEXIVOS

E.   The girl burned _____herself_____ on the stove.

1.   My young son can dress _____ very well.

2.   Can your little daughter dress _____ ?

3.   I cut _____ yesterday.

4.   Did you enjoy _____ at Mary's party last week?

5   The man shot _____ .

6.   That dog will hurt_____ if it falls in that hole.

7.   We _____ heard Peter shout at the teacher.

8.   She says that she _____ will return the book to you.

9.   I enjoyed _____ very much at the movie last night.

10. Kathy says that she also enjoyed _____

11. The soldier shot _____ with his rifle.

12. William shaves _____ every Saturday.

13. Linda hurt _____ when she fell.

14. I_____ will prepare lunch for everybody.

15. Jenny looked at _____ in the mirror.

16. We enjoyed _____ at the party last Sunday.

17. The poor woman shot _____ .

18. She cut _____ with her knife.

19. The cat hurt _____ near the fence.

20. The boy burned _____ on the stove.

LESSON 27

♦ Present Perfect Tense
♦ Affirmative Form
♦ Question Form
♦ Negative Form

PRESENT PERFECT TENSE; AFFIRMATIVE FORM

TIEMPO PRESENTE PERFECTO; FORMA AFIRMATIVA

Para formar el tiempo presente perfecto en inglés, se usa el verbo **HAVE** o **HAS** como auxiliar y se agrega el participio pasado del verbo principal. Todos los pasados participios de los verbos regulares terminan en **ED** y son iguales a la forma del tiempo pasado.

TO WORK	TRABAJAR
WORKED	**TRABAJADO**
I have worked	Yo he trabajado
You have worked	Tú has trabajado
He has worked	El ha trabajado
She has worked	Ella ha trabajado
It has worked	Ha trabajado
We have worked	Hemos trabajado
You have worked	Ustedes ha trabajado
They have worked	Ellos han trabajado

El tiempo presente perfecto se usa para describir una acción que tomó lugar en algún tiempo indefinido en el pasado.

1.	I have read that book.	Yo he leído ese libro.
2.	You have eaten a lot of rice.	Tú has comido mucho arroz.
3.	He has visited us many times.	El nos ha visitado muchas veces.
4.	She has spoken to me about that many times.	Ella me ha hablado de eso muchas veces.
5.	We have been in Boston.	Hemos estado en Boston.
6.	You have learned many new words.	Ustedes han aprendido muchas palabras nuevas.
7.	They have cleaned the house.	Ellos han limpiado la casa.

El tiempo presente perfecto también se usa para describir una acción que empezó en el pasado y continúa en el presente. En éste caso se usan generalmente las palabras **SINCE** (desde) y **FOR** (por).

1. How long have you worked here?

   ¿Cuánto tiempo has trabajado aquí?

   I have worked here for six years.

   He trabajado aquí por seis años.

2. How long have I lived here?

   ¿Por cuánto tiempo he vivido aquí?

   You have lived here since 1990.

   Tú has vivido aquí desde 1990.

3. How long has he studied English?

   ¿Por cuánto tiempo él ha estudiado inglés?

   He has studied English for five years.

   El ha estudiado inglés por cinco años.

4. How long has she been in Canada?

   ¿Por cuánto tiempo ha estado ella en Canada?

   She has been in Canada since 1987.

   Ella ha estado en Canada desde 1987.

5. How long have we taught English?

   ¿Por cuánto tiempo hemos enseñado Inglés?

   We have taught English since 1983.

   Hemos enseñado inglés desde 1983.

6. How long have we had this book?

   ¿Por cuánto tiempo hemos tenido este libro?

   You have had this book for ten years.

   Ustedes han tenido este libro por diéz años.

7. How long have they eaten rice?

   ¿Por cuánto tiempo han comido arróz?

   They have eaten rice since they were young.

   Ellos han comido arróz desde que eran jóvenes.

EJERCICIO 37	COMPLETA CON EL PRESENTE PERFECTO VEA LOS VERBOS REGULARES E IRREGULARES EN LA CUARTA PARTE

E.   (eat) You _____ have eaten _____ a lot of rice.

1.   (visit) He _____ us many times.

2.   (read) I _____ that book.

3.   (speak) She _____ to me about that many times.

4.   (be) We _____ in Boston.

5.   (learn) You _____ many new words.

6.   (clean) They _____ the house.

7.   (work) I _____ here for six years.

8.   (live) She _____ here since 1990.

9.   (be) He _____ in Canada since 1987.

10.   (study) We _____ English for five years.

11.   (teach) They _____ French since 1983.

12.   (hear) I _____ that song once or twice.

13.   (lose) She _____ her notebook.

14.   (give) Enmanuel _____ me the new calendar.

15.   (drive) We _____ to Miami from New York.

16.   (make) You _____ a lot of mistakes.

17.   (teach) Mr. Clinton _____ many students to speak English.

18.   (see) I _____ that movie three times.

19.   (read) Benny and Franklin_____ this book several times.

20.   (speak) We _____ to Mr. Lopez about the money.

PRESENT PERFECT TENSE; QUESTION FORM

TIEMPO PRESENTE PERFECTO; FORMA INTERROGATIVA

Para hacer la forma interrogativa del tiempo presente perfecto se coloca **HAVE** o **HAS** al principio de la oración.

1. Have you visited Helen this week?

   ¿Has visitado a Helen esta semana?

2. Has he read today's newspaper?

   ¿Ha leído él el periódico de hoy?

3. Has she been in New York?

   ¿Ha estado ella en New York?

4. Have they cleaned their house?

   ¿Han limpiado su casa?

5. Has John worked here since 1990?

   ¿Ha trabajado John aquí desde 1990?

6. Has Linda driven from Santiago to Santo Domingo?

   ¿Ha manejado Linda desde Santiago a Santo Domingo?

7. Have Peter and Frank studied English at the University?

   ¿Han estudiado Peter y Frank inglés en la universidad?

8. Have you seen this movie?

   ¿Has visto esta película?

PRESENT PERFECT TENSE; NEGATIVE FORM

TIEMPO PRESENTE PERFECTO; FORMA NEGATIVA

Para hacer la forma negativa del tiempo presente perfecto se coloca **NOT** después de **HAVE** o **HAS**.

TO EAT	**COMER**
EATEN	**COMIDO**
I have not eaten	Yo no he comido
You have not eaten	Tú no has comido
He has not eaten	El no ha comido
She has not eaten	Ella no ha comido
It has not eaten	No ha comido
We have not eaten	Nosotros no hemos comido
You have not eaten	Ustedes no han comdio
They have not eaten	Ellos no han comido

La contracción de **HAVE NOT** es **HAVEN'T** y de **HAS NOT** es **HASN'T**.

EJERCICIO 38 — CAMBIA A LA FORMA INTERROGATIVA Y CONTESTA EN LA FORMA NEGATIVA

E. He has worked there for a long time.

Has he worked there for a long time?

No, he hasn't worked there for a long time.

1. They have been good friends for years.

_____

_____

2. He has said that to his girlfriend.

_____

_____

3. She has known him for a long time.

_____

_____

4. John has had time to do it.

_____

_____

5. Mary has made this mistake before.

_____

_____

6. Kathy and Robert have been in London.

_____

_____

7.   All the girls have left.

_____

_____

8.   It has begun to rain.

_____

_____

9.   They have been very kind to her.

_____

_____

10.   She has lived here for ten years.

_____

_____

11.   He has been in Canada since September.

_____

_____

12.   They have known each other for a long time.

_____

_____

13.   You have spoken to her about that many times.

_____

_____

14.   She has found her pen.

_____

_____

15. The class has begun.

_____

_____

16. They have left for Mexico.

_____

_____

17. He has studied English for many years.

_____

_____

18. You have read this story.

_____

_____

19. She has worked here for about ten years.

_____

_____

20. They have finished their dinner.

_____

_____

LESSON 28

♦ Past Perfect Tense

PAST PERFECT TENSE

TIEMPO PASADO PERFECTO

El pasado perfecto se forma usando el pasado de **HAVE (HAD)** como un verbo auxiliar y agregando el pasado participio del verbo principal.

TO EAT	**COMER**
EATEN	**COMIDO**
I had eaten	Yo había comido
You had eaten	Tú habías comido
He had eaten	El había comido
She had eaten	Ella había comido
It had eaten	Había comido
We had eaten	Nosotros habíamos comido
You had eaten	Ustedes habían comido
They had eaten	Ellos habían comido

PAST PERFECT TENSE

TIEMPO PASADO PERFECTO

El pasado perfecto se usa para describir una acción que ocurrió en el pasado antes que otra acción pasada. Nunca se usa el pasado perfecto sólo, sinó siempre relacionado a alguna acción del tiempo pasado.

1.	I said that I had seen that movie.	Yo dije que yo había visto esa película.
2.	You told me that you had visited Washington several times.	Tú me dijiste que habías visitado Washington varias veces.
3.	He thought it was John who had stolen the money.	El pensó que era John quien se había robado el dinero.
4.	She saw that we had taken the wrong road.	Ella vio que habíamos tomado el camino incorrecto.
5.	He said that he had found his keys.	El dijo que había encontrado sus llaves.
6.	We told him that we had seen the movie previously.	Nosotros le dijimos que habíamos visto la película previamente.
7.	When they arrived, we had already left.	Cuando ellos llegaron, nosotros ya habíamos salido.
8.	I visited many of the places where I had played as a boy.	Yo visité muchos lugares donde había jugado cuando era un muchacho.

EJERCICIO 39   COMPLETA CON EL PASADO PERFECTO

E. (see) Frank said that he _____ had seen _____ that movie.

1. (visit) He told me that he _____ Canada many times.

2. (steal) I thought it was Peter who _____ the money.

3. (take) I saw that we _____ the wrong road.

4. (have) He said that he _____ his lunch.

5. (find) She thought that she _____ her keys.

6. (see) I told him that I _____ the movie before.

7. (leave) When we arrived, they _____.

8. (play) I visited many places where I _____ as a boy.

9. (leave) We got there just ten minutes after he _____

10. (live) He _____ there two years when the war began.

11. (see) I was sure that I _____ never _____ her before.

12. (meet) She thought that she _____ me somewhere before.

13. (break) We saw that someone _____ into that house.

14. (leave) By the time we reached there, all the guests _____.

15. (put) He said that he _____ it back where he had found it.

16. (do) She didn't say what she _____ with the money.

17. (receive) The mailman said that he _____ several packages from the United States.

18. (have) I was sure that he _____ the same problem before.

19. (take) He told us that he _____ the money to the bank.

20. (look) She said that she _____ everywhere for it.

LESSON 29

♦ Passive Voice

PASSIVE VOICE

VOZ PASIVA

La voz pasiva se forma con el verbo **TO BE** (ser, estar) como auxiliar y el pasado participio del verbo principal.

1.	The mail is delivered by John.	La correspondencia es entregada por John.
2.	This class is taught by Mary.	Esta clase es enseñada por Mary.
3.	Many articles in Spanish are written by her.	Muchos artículos en español son escritos por ella.
4.	These rooms are cleaned by the maid every day.	Estos cuartos son limpiados por la criada cada día.
5.	Dinner is prepared by Kathy every day.	La cena es preparada por Kathy cada día.
6.	Our letters are written by the President.	Nuestras cartas son escritas por el Presidente.
7.	Our compositions are corrected by the teacher.	Nuestras composiciones son corregidas por el profesor.
8.	These books are printed in the United States.	Estos libros son impresos en los Estados Unidos.

EJERCICIO 40 — CAMBIA ESTAS ORACIONES A LA VOZ PASIVA

E. John delivers the mail.

The mail is delivered by John.

1. Mary teaches this class.

_____

2. She writes many articles in Spanish.

_____

3. The maid cleans these rooms every day.

_____

4. Kathy prepares dinner every day.

_____

5. The President writes our letters.

_____

6. The teacher corrects our compositions.

_____

7. The mailman delivers the mail.

_____

8. The secretary writes all the letters.

_____

9. Frank brings the newspaper to our office.

_____

10. She brings the child to school by taxi.

_____

11. Everybody hears Kathy's speeches.

   _____

12. They print the books in Canada.

   _____

13. Everyone enjoys his speeches.

   _____

14. He cuts the grass twice a month.

   _____

15. They send the letters by airmail.

   _____

16. The lawyer prepares the contracts.

   _____

17. Mr. White provides the money for the party.

   _____

18. They sell the magazine everywhere.

   _____

19. He corrects our homework at home.

   _____

20. They deliver the mail at eight o'clock.

   _____

LESSON 30

♦ Conditional Sentences
♦ Future Possible
♦ Present Unreal
♦ Past Unreal

CONDITIONAL SENTENCES—FUTURE POSSIBLE

ORACIONES CONDICIONALES—FUTURO POSIBLE

1.	If he studies more, he will pass.	Si él estudia más, pasará.
2.	If I have time, I will visit you.	Si tengo tiempo, te visitaré.
3.	If he calls, I will tell him the truth.	Si él llama, le diré la verdad.
4.	If it rains, we will have to stay at home.	Si llueve, tendremos que quedarnos en la casa.
5.	If you don't come, I won't go to the movies.	Si tú no vienes, no iré al cine.
6.	If you attend class regularly, you will learn more English.	Si asistes regularmente a la clase, aprenderás más Inglés.
7.	If you leave early, you will get the bus.	Si sales temprano, conseguirás el autobús.
8.	If you eat a lot, you will be healthier.	Si comes mucho estarás más saludable.

CONDITIONAL SENTENCES—PRESENT UNREAL

ORACIONES CONDICIONALES—PRESENTE IRREAL

1.	If he studied more, he would pass.	Si él estudiara más, pasaría.
2.	If I had time, I would visit you.	Si tuviera tiempo, te visitaría.
3.	If he called, I would tell him the truth.	Si él llamara, le diría la verdad.
4.	If it rained, we would have to stay at home.	Si lloviera, tendríamos que quedarnos en la casa.
5.	If you didn't come, I wouldn't go to the movies.	Si tú no vinieras, no iría al cine.
6.	If you attended class regularly, you would learn more English.	Si asistieras regularmente a clase, aprenderías más Inglés.
7.	If you left early, you would get the bus.	Si salieras temprano, conseguirías el autobús.
8.	If you ate a lot, you would be healthier.	Si comieras mucho, estarías más saludable.

CONDITIONAL SENTENCES—PAST UNREAL

ORACIONES CONDICIONALES—PASADO IRREAL

1.	If he had studied more, he would have passed.	Si él hubiera estudiado más, habría pasado.
2.	If I had had time, I would have visited you.	Si hubiera tenido tiempo, te habria visitado.
3.	If he had called, I would have told him the truth.	Si él hubiera llamado, le habría dicho la verdad.
4.	If it had rained, we would have had to stay at home.	Si hubiera llovido, habríamos tenido que quedarnos en la casa.
5.	If you hadn't come, I wouldn't have gone to the movies.	Si tú no hubieras venido, no hubiera ido al cine.
6.	If you had attended class regularly, you would have learned more English.	Si tú hubieras asistido regularmente a clase, habrías aprendido más Inglés.
7.	If you had left early, you would have gotten the bus.	Si hubieras salido temprano, habrías conseguido el autobús.
8.	If you had eaten a lot, you would have been healthier.	Si tú hubieras comido mucho, habrías estado más saludable.

EJERCICIO 41

COMPLETA CON LA FORMA CORRECTA DEL VERBO

E.   (study) If Mary _____ studies _____ hard, she will pass.

1.   (have) If I _____ time, I will visit you.

2.   (hurry) If she _____, she will get the bus.

3.   (rain) If it _____, we won't go to the beach.

4.   (come) If Peter_____, he can help us.

5.   (attend) If you _____class regularly, you will learn English very much.

6.   (see) If I _____her, I will give her your message.

7.   (leave) If they _____early, they can get there on time.

8.   (spend) If John _____more time on his lessons, he would get better marks.

9.   (call) If he _____, I would tell him the truth.

10. (rain) If it _____, we would have to stay at home.

11. (work) If she _____harder, she would get a better position.

12. (know) If I _____her telephone number, I would call her.

13. (speak) If you _____French well, you would take a trip to France.

14. (go) If he _____to bed earlier, he would be less tired.

15. (pay) If she _____more attention in class, she would have passed the course.

16. (study) If you _____languages, it would have been easier for you to travel.

17. (know) If I _____you were waiting for me, I would have hurried to get there.

18. (go) If you _____with us, you would have seen a good show.

19. (tell) If she _____me the truth, I would have been less angry.

20. (see) If I _____him, I would have given him your message.

EJERCICIO 42

COMPLETA CON LA FORMA CORRECTA DEL VERBO

E   (pass) If Kathy studies hard, she __will pass__ her exams.

1.   (visit) If I have time next week, I_____ you.

2.   (go) If it doesn't rain, we_____ to the beach.

3.   (get) If you leave early, you_____ the bus.

4.   (be) If she eats more, she_____ healthier.

5.   (let) If I decide to go to the movies, I_____ you know.

6.   (drive) If I get a car, I_____ to the mountains.

7.   (take) If we have enough money, we_____ a trip to Canada.

8.   (play) If I knew how to play the piano, I_____ for my friends.

9.   (speak) If Paul had more practice, he_____ better English.

10.   (have) If he knew how to drive, he_____ fewer accidents.

11.   (study) If she liked languages, she_____ English and German.

12.   (go) If Michael had the time, he_____ to New York.

13.   (make) If we studied together, we_____ more progress.

14.   (walk) If I lived near, I_____ to school every day.

15.   (call) If I had your telephone number, I_____ you.

16.   (go) If yesterday had been a holiday, we_____ to the beach.

17.   (catch) If they had left earlier, they_____ the bus.

18.   (give) If you had seen her, you_____ her my message.

19.   (get) If he had had more experience, he_____ the job.

20.   (meet) If you had gone with us, you_____ her.

SEGUNDA PARTE

Respuestas A Los Ejercicios

ANSWERS TO THE EXERCISES

EJERCICIO 1		EJERCICIO 2	
1.	A	1.	Tables
2.	An	2.	Porches
3.	A	3.	Boxes
4.	An	4.	Books
5.	An	5.	Bosses
6.	A	6.	Pens
7.	An	7.	Men
8.	An	8.	Feet
9.	A	9.	Tomatoes
10.	An	10.	Buses
11.	A	11.	Kisses
12.	An	12.	Churches
13.	A	13.	Women
14.	A	14.	Children
15.	An	15.	Teeth
16.	An	16.	Teachers
17.	A	17.	Houses
18.	A	18.	Mice
19.	An	19.	Potatoes
20.	A	20.	Lessons

	EJERCICIO 3		EJERCICIO 4
1.	This	1.	That
2.	This	2.	Those
3.	These	3.	Those
4.	This	4.	Those
5.	These	5.	That
6.	These	6.	That
7.	This	7.	That
8.	These	8.	Those
9.	This	9.	That
10.	This	10.	Those
11.	These	11.	That
12.	This	12.	Those
13.	These	13.	That
14.	This	14.	That
15.	This	15.	Those
16.	These	16.	Those
17.	These	17.	That
18.	This	18.	That
19.	These	19.	Those
20.	This	20.	That

	EJERCICIO 5		EJERCICIO 6
1.	These pens	1.	am
2.	Those tables	2.	is
3.	These pencils	3.	is
4.	Those schools	4.	are
5.	These pages	5.	are
6.	These cars	6.	is
7.	Those men	7.	is
8.	These houses	8.	is
9.	Those pictures	9.	is
10.	Those women	10.	are
11.	These children	11.	are
12.	These classes	12.	are
13.	Those words	13.	are
14.	Those stores	14.	is
15.	Those dresses	15.	is
16.	These lessons	16.	is
17.	Those students	17.	are
18.	Those boxes	18.	are
19.	These countries	19.	am
20.	Those questions	20.	are

	EJERCICIO 7
1.	Are you a student?
2.	Is he a mechanic?
3.	Is she a nurse?
4.	Is it a dog?
5.	Are we professionals?
6.	Are you students?
7.	Are they teachers?
8.	Are we cousins?
9.	Is he a bad student?
10.	Is today Tuesday?
11.	Are John and Christopher in the same class?
12.	Are you and George cousins?
13.	Are she and Mary good friends?
14.	Is the door open?
15.	Is the window closed?
16.	Are they new students?
17.	Are we busy today?
18.	Are Mr. Smith and Mrs. White Americans?
19.	Is this a difficult exercise?
20.	Is that a good book?

	EJERCICIO 8
1.	You are not a teacher.
2.	He is not a pilot.
3.	She is not a secretary.
4.	It is not a car.
5.	We are not mechanics.
6.	You are not lawyers.
7.	They are not policemen.
8.	He is not happy.
9.	She is not pretty.
10.	You are not from Europe.
11.	Mary is not very happy.
12.	They are not ready now.
13.	The boy is not small.
14.	The house is not big.
15.	They are not students here.
16.	Mr. Brown is not busy now.
17.	English is not very difficult.
18.	Mary and Helen are not students.
19.	This English book is not expensive.
20.	The children are not in the house.

Prof. Benjamin Franklin Arias, Ph.D.

	EJERCICIO 9
1.	Today isn't Monday.
2.	She and Mary aren't sisters.
3.	This isn't a difficult exercise.
4.	He isn't a good student.
5.	Mr. Lara isn't a good teacher.
6.	Peter and John aren't Americans.
7.	She isn't a good friend.
8.	They aren't busy today.
9.	You and Henry aren't cousins.
10.	Joseph and I aren't in the same class.
11.	William isn't busy today.
12.	You aren't a good student.
13.	You and George aren't good friends.
14.	Mary and I aren't good friends.
15.	The door isn't closed.
16.	The blue windows aren't open.
17.	They aren't brothers.
18.	We aren't friends.
19.	They aren't new students.
20.	He isn't a good doctor.

	EJERCICIO 10		EJERCICIO 11
1.	There are	1.	have
2.	There are	2.	has
3.	There is	3.	has
4.	There are	4.	has
5.	There are	5.	have
6.	There are	6.	have
7.	There is	7.	have
8.	There are	8.	has
9.	There are	9.	have
10.	There is	10.	have
11.	There are	11.	have
12.	There is	12.	has
13.	There are	13.	has
14.	There are	14.	have
15.	There are	15.	has
16.	There is	16.	has
17.	There is	17.	have
18.	There are	18.	have
19.	There is	19.	have
20.	There is	20.	has

	EJERCICIO 12	
1.	Does she have many friends in our class?	No, she doesn't have many friends in our class.
2.	Do you have a new pen?	No, I don't have a new pen.
3.	Does he have three English classes a week?	No, he doesn't have three English classes a week.
4.	Do they have a new car.	No, they don't have a new car.
5.	Do we have a good time at the party?	No, we don't have a good time at the party.
6.	Does John have an English class every day?	No, he doesn't have an English class every day.
7.	Do they have their vacation in July?	No, they don't have their vacation in July.
8.	Does she have two brothers and one sister?	No, she doesn't have two brothers and one sister.
9.	Do we have many new words to learn today?	No, we don't have many new words to learn today.
10.	Does Helen have a new hat?	No, she doesn't have a new hat.
11.	Do you have a red shirt?	No, I don't have a red shirt.
12.	Do we have our English class in Room 5?	No, we don't have our English class in Room 5.
13.	Does she have a bad cold?	No, she doesn't have a bad cold.
14.	Does Frank have a headache?	No, he doesn't have a headache.
15.	Do they have a new television set?	No, they don't have a new television set.
16.	Do we have many friends in New York?	No, we don't have many friends in New York.
17.	Does that dog have a very long tail?	No, it doesn't have a very long tail.
18.	Does the teacher have brown hair?	No, he doesn't have brown hair.
19.	Does this book have a blue cover?	No, it doesn't have a blue cover.
20.	Does he have many English books?	No, he doesn't have many English books.

	EJERCICIO 13		EJERCICIO 14
1.	write	1.	Does the boy know the answer?
2.	goes	2.	Do the girls work in a store?
3.	sit	3.	Do you know many new words?
4.	opens	4.	Does John study very hard?
5.	works	5.	Do they go to school every day?
6.	smokes	6.	Does she ask many questions?
7.	kisses	7.	Do we spend a lot of money?
8.	read	8.	Does Mr. Arias speak very fast?
9.	eats	9.	Do you understand the lesson?
10.	play	10.	Do they write many letters?
11.	washes	11.	Does he know many English words?
12.	carries	12.	Does Mary speak English very well?
13.	try	13.	Do the boys like coffee?
14.	studies	14.	Do the women come from Canada?
15.	puts	15.	Does Mr. Brown teach English?
16.	watches	16.	Does Helen live in New York?
17.	bring	17.	Does that student study every day?
18.	fixes	18.	Does the baby cry very much?
19.	prepare	19.	Does he write letters every day?
20.	leaves	20.	Do they go to Mexico every year?

	EJERCICIO 15		EJERCICIO 16
1.	He doesn't understand that lesson.	1.	his
2.	They don't go to school every day.	2.	her
3.	She doesn't ask many questions.	3.	my
4.	Frank doesn't write many letters.	4.	our
5.	The men don't come from Brazil.	5.	my
6.	The tall woman doesn't speak very fast.	6.	her
7.	That boy doesn't work very hard.	7.	our
8.	I don't study the lesson every day.	8.	their
9.	Those people don't like coffee.	9.	their
10.	They don't speak French well.	10.	his
11.	Those boys don't live in Chicago.	11.	his
12.	Mr. Smith doesn't teach English.	12.	my
13.	We don't know many English words.	13.	its
14.	John and William don't have many friends.	14.	its
15.	They don't spend a lot of money.	15.	my
16.	She doesn't study every afternoon.	16.	her
17.	He doesn't speak that language.	17.	their
18.	Mr. Brown doesn't work very hard.	18.	your
19.	The new students don't understand this.	19.	their
20.	Mr. Lopez doesn't fly to England every year.	20.	our

	EJERCICIO 17	
1.	You have to go to the hospital.	You don't have to go to the hospital
2.	He has to eat more.	He doesn't have to eat more.
3.	She has to dance with me.	She doesn't have to dance with me.
4.	It has to be at three o'clock.	It doesn't have to be at three o'clock.
5.	We have to speak English.	We don't have to speak English.
6.	You have to write sentences.	You don't have to write sentences.
7.	They have to eat bananas.	They don't have to eat bananas.
8.	Kathy has to come to class every day.	Kathy doesn't have to come to class every day.
9.	Lisa has to go to the hospital.	Lisa doesn't have to go to the hospital.
10.	She has to write many letters.	She doesn't have to write many letters.
11.	He has to buy many books.	He doesn't have to buy many books.
12.	I have to read the newspaper every morning.	I don't have to read the newspaper every morning.
13.	She has to drink milk with her meals.	She doesn't have to drink milk with her meals.
14.	He has to eat lunch in the cafeteria.	He doesn't have to eat lunch in the cafeteria.
15.	I have to get up early every morning.	I don't have to get up early every morning.
16.	They have to speak English in Canada.	They don't have to speak English in Canada.
17.	She has to come to school by bus.	She doesn't have to come to school by bus.
18.	We have to speak Spanish every day.	We don't have to speak Spanish every day.
19.	He has to eat dinner at home.	He doesn't have to eat dinner at home.
20.	They have to read many English books.	They don't have to read many English books.

	EJERCICIO 18
1.	I often go to the movies with her.
2.	I like them very much.
3.	He never speaks to us.
4.	We also like them very much.
5.	She writes many letters to her.
6.	I sit near them.
7.	We see her in the cafeteria every day.
8.	I understand him very well.
9.	He gives him a lot of money.
10.	She always speaks to her in English.
11.	He sends her many presents.
12.	Mark writes many letters to her.
13.	I sit near them in the classroom.
14.	Kathy sits near them.
15.	We write many letters to them.
16.	She sees you on the bus every morning.
17.	I often see them in the cafeteria.
18.	I know them very well.
19.	They usually go to the movies with them.
20.	She wants to go to the party with us.

	EJERCICIO 19
1.	Don't come back at two o'clock.
2.	Don't sit in that chair.
3.	Don't open the window.
4.	Don't close the door.
5.	Don't stand up.
6.	Please don't go.
7.	Don't ask Mr. Smith to come in.
8.	Don't take the next bus.
9.	Don't wait on that corner.
10.	Don't put your books there on that desk.
11.	Don't hang your coat on that chair.
12.	Don't study the next lesson.
13.	Don't write all the exercises in this lesson.
14.	Don't help Frank with his lesson.
15.	Don't speak English in this class.
16.	Don't give this to Mr.Brown.
17.	Don't sit in the sun.
18.	Don't drive fast.
19.	Don't tell Mary to wait for us.
20.	Don't put these chairs in the next room.

	EJERCICIO 20		EJERCICIO 21
1.	are dancing	1.	was
2.	is writing	2.	was
3.	is coming	3.	was
4.	is drinking	4.	were
5.	are learning	5.	were
6.	are eating	6.	was
7.	are dancing	7.	were
8.	is pushing	8.	was
9.	is pulling	9.	was
10.	is preparing	10.	were
11.	is waiting	11.	was
12.	is beginning	12.	was
13.	are taking	13.	was
14.	are making	14.	were
15.	is ringing	15.	was
16.	are studying	16.	were
17.	is leaving	17.	were
18.	is looking	18.	were
19.	is knocking	19.	was
20.	is reading	20.	were

	EJERCICIO 22		EJERCICIO 23
1.	were dancing	1.	lived
2.	was writing	2.	walked
3.	was coming	3.	watched
4.	was drinking	4.	smoked
5.	were learning	5.	washed
6.	were eating	6.	liked
7.	were dancing	7.	stopped
8.	was pushing	8.	listened
9.	was pulling	9.	rained
10.	was studying	10.	waited
11.	were playing	11.	felt
12.	was giving	12.	drank
13.	were talking	13.	wore
14.	was looking	14.	read
15.	was counting	15.	left
16.	were studying	16.	rode
17.	was hitting	17.	bought
18.	was running	18.	saw
19.	were repeating	19.	taught
20.	were smiling	20.	heard

	EJERCICIO 24
1.	Did he sell the car?
2.	Did John buy a new pair of shoes?
3.	Did he speak to the girl after class?
4.	Did she say anything interesting?
5.	Did they go to the baseball game?
6.	Did she bring a friend to school?
7.	Did Mr. Lopez wear a new shirt?
8.	Did the students come at eight o'clock?
9.	Did he make a mistake on the test?
10.	Did the boys hold the box carefully?
11.	Did Frank write the answer on the paper?
12.	Did Tommy and Peter eat any sandwiches?
13.	Did you drink too much coffee last night?
14.	Did they feel very bad this morning?
15.	Did the train leave at 5:30 P.M.?
16.	Did Mary choose a pretty skirt?
17.	Did Mr. Arias teach English last year?
18.	Did Benny put the money in his wallet?
19.	Did we find the purse on the floor?
20.	Did they hear that radio program?

	EJERCICIO 25
1.	Should he wait on that corner?
2.	May I smoke here?
3.	Must he go out of town?
4.	Would you like to go to the movies?
5.	Could I meet you at two o'clock?
6.	Can she go with us tonight?
7.	Should we tell Helen about it?
8.	May I wait in Mary's office?
9.	Must they explain it to him?
10.	Could you wait in his office?
11.	May we sit here?
12.	Would you like to drink coffee?
13.	Should he stay at home?
14.	Can she meet us after dinner?
15.	Must you write him a letter?
16.	May I wait here?
17.	Should she sit near the window?
18.	Can John play the violin well?
19.	Would you like to swim today?
20.	Must she go tomorrow?

	EJERCICIO 26
1.	He should not speak Spanish in the classroom.
2.	You may not smoke here.
3.	She must not see him.
4.	I can not call her later.
5.	We would not like to go on foot.
6.	They could not see the movie.
7.	You should not tell her about it.
8.	We may not open the window.
9.	I must not tell John about the problem.
10.	She can not play the piano very well.
11.	I would not like to wash the car.
12.	We could not do all of these exercises.
13.	They should not be back before noon.
14.	Janet may not go to the party with us.
15.	We must not do that again.
16.	They can not meet us later.
17.	She would not like to clean the house.
18.	I could not understand her well.
19.	He should not sit near the window.
20.	You may not come in now.

	EJERCICIO 27	
1.	He will study in this class.	He is going to study in this class.
2.	She will work in this office.	She is going to work in this office.
3.	You will speak English very well.	You are going to speak English very well.
4.	I will come to the lesson on time.	I am going to come to the lesson on time.
5.	They will walk to their work.	They are going to walk to their work.
6.	He will bring his friends to the class.	He is going to bring his friends to the class.
7.	She will open the door for us.	She is going to open the door for us.
8.	They will study very much.	They are going to study very much.
9.	She will bring all her books to the lesson.	She is going to bring all her books to the lesson.
10.	He will play the violin very well.	He is going to play the violin very well.
11.	We will carry all the small packages.	We are going to carry all the small packages.
12.	She will speak to us in English.	She is going to speak to us in English.
13.	He will write a letter to his mother every day.	He is going to write a letter to his mother every day.
14.	I will bring you many presents.	I am going to bring you many presents.
15.	She will arrive to the classroom on time.	She is going to arrive to the classroom on time.
16.	He will work from nine to five.	He is going to work from nine to five.
17.	They will eat all their meals in the cafeteria.	They are going to eat all their meals in the cafeteria.
18.	The train will leave at eight o'clock.	The train is going to leave at eight o'clock.
19.	You will like that teacher very much.	You are going to like that teacher very much.
20.	She will teach us English and Mathematics.	She is going to teach us English and Mathematics.

	EJERCICIO 28		EJERCICIO 29
1.	What	1.	How much
2.	Where	2.	How many
3.	When	3.	How many
4.	How	4.	How much
5.	Why	5.	How many
6.	What	6.	How much
7.	Where	7.	How much
8.	When	8.	How many
9.	How	9.	How many
10.	Why	10.	How much
11.	What	11.	How many
12.	Where	12.	How much
13.	When	13.	How many
14.	How	14.	How much
15.	Why	15.	How many
16.	What	16.	How much
17.	Where	17.	How many
18.	When	18.	How much
19.	How	19.	How many
20.	Why	20.	How much

	EJERCICIO 30		EJERCICIO 31
1.	beautiful	1.	sweeter
2.	soft	2.	warmer
3.	softly	3.	more interesting
4.	cleverly	4.	easier
5.	clever	5.	more intelligent
6.	carefully	6.	colder
7.	careful	7.	larger
8.	slow	8.	longer
9.	slowly	9.	busier
10.	quickly	10.	wider
11.	easy	11.	shorter
12.	easily	12.	more peaceful
13.	frequently	13.	higher
14.	frequent	14.	more beautiful
15.	serious	15.	later
16.	seriously	16.	sooner
17.	carelessly	17.	earlier
18.	careless	18.	faster
19.	foolish	19.	deeper
20.	foolishly	20.	faster

	EJERCICIO 32		EJERCICIO 33
1.	most comfortable	1.	any
2.	easiest	2.	some
3.	largest	3.	some
4.	most expensive	4.	any
5.	youngest	5.	any
6.	coldest	6.	some
7.	most intelligent	7.	any
8.	largest	8.	any
9.	tallest	9.	some
10.	prettiest	10.	any
11.	busiest	11.	any
12.	widest	12.	some
13.	most difficult	13.	some
14.	tallest	14.	any
15.	most beautiful	15.	any
16.	largest	16.	any
17.	most intelligent	17.	some
18.	longest	18.	some
19.	easiest	19.	some
20.	fastest	20.	any

	EJERCICIO 34		EJERCICIO 35
1.	too	1.	These pencils are mine.
2.	very	2.	This office is his.
3.	too	3.	These magazines are ours.
4.	too	4.	These books are mine.
5.	very	5.	Those pictures on the table are yours.
6.	too	6.	These pens are theirs.
7.	very	7.	I think that this notebook is yours.
8.	too	8.	This newspaper is mine.
9.	very	9.	This clock is hers.
10.	too	10.	That hat is his.
11.	too	11.	This umbrella is ours.
12.	very	12.	These seats are theirs.
13.	too	13.	That pair of shoes is hers.
14.	too	14.	This classroom is mine.
15.	very	15.	That chair is his.
16.	too	16.	These books are ours.
17.	too	17.	Those calendars over there on the desk are theirs.
18.	too	18.	This eraser is yours.
19.	too	19.	That table in this room is mine.
20.	very	20.	These English books are his.

	EJERCICIO 36		EJERCICIO 37
1.	himself	1.	has visited
2.	herself	2.	have read
3.	myself	3.	has spoken
4.	yourself	4.	have been
5.	himself	5.	have learned
6.	itself	6.	have cleaned
7.	ourselves	7.	have worked
8.	herself	8.	has lived
9.	myself	9.	has been
10.	herself	10.	have studied
11.	himself	11.	have taught
12.	himself	12.	have heard
13.	herself	13.	has lost
14.	myself	14.	has given
15.	herself	15.	have driven
16.	ourselves	16.	have made
17.	herself	17.	has taught
18.	herself	18.	have seen
19.	itself	19.	have read
20.	himself	20.	have spoken

EJERCICIO 38

1.	Have they been good friends for years?	No, they haven't been good friends for years.
2.	Has he said that to his girlfriend?	No, he hasn't said that to his girlfriend.
3.	Has she known him for a long time?	No, she hasn't known him for a long time.
4.	Has John had time to do it?	No, he hasn't had time to do it.
5.	Has Mary made this mistake before?	No, she hasn't made this mistake before.
6.	Have Kathy and Robert been in London?	No, they haven't been in London.
7.	Have all the girls left?	No, the girls haven't left.
8.	Has it begun to rain?	No, it hasn't begun to rain.
9.	Have they been very kind to her?	No, they haven't been very kind to her.
10.	Has she lived here for ten years?	No, she hasn't lived here for ten years.
11.	Has he been in Canada since September?	No, he hasn't been in Canada since September.
12.	Have they known each other for a long time?	No, they haven't known each other for a long time.
13.	Have you spoken to her about that many times?	No, I haven't spoken to her about that many times.
14.	Has she found her pen?	No, she hasn't found her pen.
15.	Has the class begun?	No, it hasn't begun.
16.	Have they left for Mexico?	No, they haven't left for Mexico.
17.	Has he studied English for many years?	No, he hasn't studied English for many years.
18.	Have you read this story?	No, I haven't read this story.
19.	Has she worked here for about ten years?	No, she hasn't worked here for about ten years.
20.	Have they finished their dinner?	No, they haven't finished their dinner.

	EJERCICIO 39		EJERCICIO 40
1.	had visited	1.	This class is taught by Mary.
2.	had stolen	2.	Many articles in Spanish are written by her.
3.	had taken	3.	These rooms are cleaned by the maid every day.
4.	had had	4.	Dinner is prepared by Kathy every day.
5.	had found	5.	Our letters are written by the President.
6.	had seen	6.	Our compositions are corrected by the teacher.
7.	had left	7.	The mail is delivered by the mailman.
8.	had played	8.	All the letters are written by the secretary.
9.	had left	9.	The newspaper is brought by Frank to our office.
10.	had lived	10.	The child is brought by her to school by taxi.
11.	had never seen	11.	Kathy's speeches are heard by everybody.
12.	had met	12.	The books are printed by them in Canada.
13.	had broken	13.	His speeches are enjoyed by everyone.
14.	had left	14.	The grass is cut by him twice a month.
15.	had put	15.	The letters are sent by them by airmail.
16.	had done	16.	The contracts are prepared by the lawyer.
17.	had received	17.	The money for the party is provided by Mr. White.
18.	had had	18.	The magazine is sold by them everywhere.
19.	had taken	19.	Our homework is corrected by him at home.
20.	had looked	20.	The mail is delivered by them at eight o'clock.

	EJERCICIO 41		EJERCICIO 42
1.	have	1.	will visit
2.	hurries	2.	will go
3.	rains	3.	will get
4.	comes	4.	will be
5.	attend	5.	will let
6.	see	6.	will drive
7.	leave	7.	will take
8.	spent	8.	would play
9.	called	9.	would speak
10.	rained	10.	would have
11.	worked	11.	would study
12.	knew	12.	would go
13.	spoke	13.	would make
14.	went	14.	would walk
15.	had paid	15.	would call
16.	had studied	16.	would have gone
17.	had known	17.	would have caught
18.	had gone	18.	would have given
19.	had told	19.	would have gotten
20.	had seen	20.	would have met

TERCERA PARTE

Temas Misceláneos

TEMAS MISCELANEOS

- ◆ Definite Article
- ◆ Contractions
- ◆ Adverbs
- ◆ Conjunctions
- ◆ Interjections
- ◆ Prepositions
- ◆ Numbers
- ◆ Colors
- ◆ Days
- ◆ Months
- ◆ Seasons

DEFINITE ARTICLE

ARTICULO DEFINIDO

El artículo definido es **THE** (el, la, los, las) y se emplea antes de nombres que indiquen personas o cosas determinadas o específicas.

1.	The dress	El vestido
2.	The dresses	Los vestidos

No se usa el artículo definido:
a) Antes de un nombre no modificado que indique una cualidad, condición o sensación (nombre abstracto) ni antes de nombres usados en sentido general, es decir, cuando abarcan todos los de su especie sin especificar grupo.

1.	Kindness is beautiful.	La bondad es hermosa.
2.	Life is trying at times.	La vida es dura a veces.
3.	Hunger is the best sauce.	A buena hambre no hay pan duro.
		(El hambre es la mejor salsa).
4.	Dogs are faithful.	Los perros son fieles.
5.	Coal is very useful.	El carbón es muy útil.
6.	Bread is very cheap now.	El pan es muy barato ahora.
7.	Sunday is a day of rest.	El Domingo es un día de descanso.

b) Antes de títulos si estos van seguidos de nombres propios o apellidos.

1.	President Clark is in favor of the plan.	El presidente Clark está en favor del plan.
2.	Secretary Hull is honest and sincere.	El Secretario Hull es honrado y sincero.
3.	Lieutenant Johnson is not a big man.	El Teniente Johnson no es un hombre grande

c)   Antes de nombres de comidas y calles.

    1.   After breakfast.   Después del desayuno.
    2.   After lunch.   Después del almuerzo.
    3.   Before dinner.   Antes de la cena.
    4.   For supper.   Para la cena.
    5.   On Duarte Street.   En la calle Duarte.

d)   Antes de un nombre propio de persona modificado.

    Poor Mary is very ill.   La pobre María esta muy enferma.

e)   Antes de nombres de idiomas no modificados.

    1   English and Spanish are   El Inglés y el Español son muy
         very necessary.   necesarios.
    2.   I am learning French.   Yo estoy aprendiendo el Francés.

f)   Antes de la palabra "last" significando "pasado" y de "next" significando "próximo".

    1.   Last week   La semana pasada
    2.   Last month   El mes pasado
    3.   Last night   Anoche
    4.   Next Sunday   El próximo Domingo
    5.   Next year   El próximo año.

g)   Antes de las palabras school (escuela), college (colegio), church (iglesia), jail (cárcel).

    1.   I am going to school.   Voy para la escuela.
    2.   My children are at school. Mis niños están en la escuela.
    3.   They are taking him to jail. Se lo están llevando para la cárcel.

CONTRACTIONS

CONTRACCIONES

Las contracciones son muy comunes en inglés, especialmente en el lenguaje coloquial y la escritura familiar. Consisten en hacer una sola sílaba o palabra al unir pronombres, nombres, adverbios, palabras interrogativas, la negación NOT, con el verbo o auxiliar.

a)   Contracciones con pronombres

I am	I'm
You are	You're
He is	He's
She is	She's
It is	It's
We are	We're
They are	They're
That is	That's
I have	I've
You have	You've
He has	He's
She has	she's
It has	It's
We have	We've
They have	They've

Las contracciones con el verbo o auxiliar TO HAVE solamente se usan con los participios pasados de otros verbos, en estos casos TO HAVE se traduce HABER.

She's written a book.   Ella ha escrito un libro.

No se usan las contracciones en los casos en que TO HAVE se traduce TENER.

She has a book.	Ella tiene un libro.
I had	I'd
You had	You'd
He had	He'd
She had	She'd
We had	We'd
They had	They'd
I will	I'll
You will	You'll
He will	He'll
She Will	She'll
It will	It'll
We will	We'll
They will	They'll
That will	That'll
I would	I'd
You would	You'd
He would	He'd
She would	She'd
We would	We'd
They would	They'd

b) Contracciones con substantivos o nombres

1. John's sick. — John está enfermo.
2. Kathy's a good secretary. — Kathy es una buena secretaria.
3. My friend's going to Canada. — Mi amigo va para Canada.
4. Three's a crowd. — Aquí sobra uno.

    (Literalmente: Tres es un gentío).

c) Contracciones con adverbios

Here is	Here's
There is	There's
There will	There'll
There would	There'd

d) Contracciones con palabras interrogativas

How is	How's
What is	What's
When is	When's
Where is	Where's
Who is	Who's
What has	What's
Who has	Who's
Who had	Who'd
What will	What'll
Who will	Who'll
Who would	Who'd

e) Contracciones negativas

are not	aren't
is not	isn't
was not	wasn't
were not	weren't
have not	haven't
has not	hasn't
had not	hadn't
do not	don't
does not	doesn't
did not	didn't
will not	won't
would not	wouldn't

shall not	shan't
should not	shouldn't
can not	can't
cannot	can't
could not	couldn't
might not	mightn't
must not	mustn't

En los siguientes casos las contracciones pueden hacerse en dos formas.

You are not	You're not	You aren't
He is not	He's not	He isn't
You have not	You've not	You haven't

ADVERBS OF MODE

ADVERBIOS DE MODO

---

aloud	en voz alta
how	como
scarcely	apenas
slowly	despacio
so	así
softly	suavemente
strictly	en rigor
thus	así
truly	de veras
well	bién

ADVERBS OF PLACE

ADVERBIOS DE LUGAR

afar	lejos
anywhere	en alguna parte
around	alrededor
away	fuera
backward	hacia atrás
below	abajo
behind	atrás
elsewhere	en otra parte
far	lejos
forward	adelante
here	aquí
in	en
near	cerca
nowhere	en ninguna parte
off	fuera
somewhere	en alguna parte
there	allí, ahí
up	arriba
upward	hacia arriba
where	dónde

ADVERBS OF QUANTITY

ADVERBIOS DE CANTIDAD

almost	casi
enough	bastante
entirely	del todo

little	poco
more	más
mostly	mayormente
much	mucho
nearly	por poco
too	demasiado
too much	demasiado
very	muy

ADVERBS OF TIME

ADVERBIOS DE TIEMPO

---

already	ya
always	siempre
at last	al fín
afterwards	después
again	otra vez
before	antes
ever	siempre
forever	para siempre
frequently	frecuentemente
immediately	inmediatamente
instantly	al instante
never	nunca
now	ahora
often	a menudo
once	una vez
seldom	rara vez
soon	pronto
sometimes	algunas veces
suddenly	de repente
today	hoy

while	mientras
yet	todavía

CONJUNCTIONS

CONJUNCIONES

after	después de
although	aunque
and	y
as…as	tan…como
because	porque
before	antes de
but	pero
either…or	o…o
if	si
lest	a no ser que
neither…nor	ni…ni
nevertheless	sin embargo
no only…but	no solo…pero
not so…as	no tan…como
so…that	tan…que
that	que
though	aunque
till	hasta
unless	a menos que
until	hasta que
when	cuando
when ever	cuando sea
whereas	considerando
whether…or	si…o
while	mientras
yet, however	sin embargo

INTERJECTIONS

INTERJECCIONES

1. **De dolor**
   Ouch! Ah! ¡ay!
2. **De alegría**
   Cheer up! ¡animo!
3. **De admiración**
   How beautiful! ¡Que hermosa!
   Indeed! ¡De veras!
   Really! ¡De veras!
   Look here! ¡Mire!
   Strange! ¡Es extrano!
4. **De desprecio**
   Pshaw! ¡Bah!
5. **De disgusto**
   Away! ¡Fuera!
   Begone! ¡Vayase!
   Get out! ¡Fuera de aquí!
6. **Para llamar la atención**
   Beware! ¡Cuidada!
   Look out! ¡Cuidado!
7. **Para imponer silencio**
   Silence! ¡Silencio!
8. **Para saludar**
   Hello! ¡Hola!
   Welcome! ¡Bienvenido!
9. **Para expresar otros sentimientos**
   Bravo! ¡Bravo!
   Forward! ¡Adelante!
   Good heavens! ¡Santo cielo!
   Never mind! ¡Que importa!

| Nonsense! | ¡Tontería! |
| What a pity! | ¡Que lastima! |

PREPOSITIONS

PREPOSICIONES

---

about	cerca, sobre
above	sobre, encima
across	a través
after	después
against	contra
among	entre
around	alrededor
at	en
before	antes, delante
behind	detrás, atrás
below	bajo, debajo de
beneath	bajo, debajo de
between	entre
beyond	más allá
by	por
except	excepto
for	por, para
from	de, desde
in	en, dentro
into	en, dentro
of	de
off	fuera
on	sobre, encima
out	fuera
over	arriba, sobre
regarding	tocante a

PREPOSITIONS

PREPOSICIONES (CONTINUACION)

since	desde que
through	por, a través
till	hasta
to	a, para
towards	hacia
under	debajo de
underneath	debajo
until	hasta
up	arriba
upon	sobre
with	con
within	dentro de
without	sin

CARDINAL NUMBERS

NUMEROS CARDINALES

0	zero
1	one
2	two
3	three
4	four
5	five
6	six
7	seven
8	eight
9	nine

10	ten
11	eleven
12	twelve
13	thirteen
14	fourteen
15	fifteen
16	sixteen
17	seventeen
18	eighteen
19	nineteen
20	twenty
21	twenty-one
22	twenty-two
30	thirty
31	thirty-one
40	forty
50	fifty
60	sixty
70	seventy
80	eighty
90	ninety
100	one hundred
101	one hundred one
102	one hundred two
200	two hundred
300	three hundred
400	four hundred
1000	one thousand
2000	two thousand
50,000	fifty thousand
100,000	one hundred thousand
1,000,000	one million
100,000,000	one hundred million
1, 000,000,000	one billion

ORDINAL NUMBERS

NUMEROS ORDINALES

first	primero
second	segundo
third	tercero
fourth	cuarto
fifth	quinto
sixth	sexto
seventh	séptimo
eighth	octavo
nineth	noveno
tenth	décimo
eleventh	undécimo
twelfth	duodécimo
thirteenth	decimotercero
fourteenth	decimocuarto
fifteenth	decimoquinto
sixteenth	decimosexto
seventeenth	decimoseptimo
eighteenth	decimoctavo
nineteenth	decimonoveno
twentieth	vigésimo
twenty-first	vigesimoprimero
thirtieth	trigésimo
fortieth	cuadragésimo
fiftieth	quincuagésimo
sixtieth	sexagésimo
seventieth	septuagésimo
eightieth	octagésimo
ninetieth	nonagésimo
hundredth	centésimo

hundred first	centésimo primero
thousandth	milésimo

COLORS

COLORES

black	negro
blue	azul
brown	marrón
dark	oscuro
flashy	chillón
green	verde
light	claro
pink	rosado
red	rojo
white	blanco
yellow	amarillo

DAY OF THE WEEK

DIAS DE LA SEMANA

Sunday	Domingo
Monday	Lunes
Tuesday	Martes
Wednesday	Miércoles
Thursday	Jueves
Friday	Viernes
Saturday	Sábado

MONTHS OF THE YEAR

MESES DEL AÑO

January	enero
February	febrero
March	marzo
April	abril
May	mayo
June	junio
July	julio
August	agosto
September	septiembre
October	octubre
November	noviembre
December	diciembre

SEASONS OF THE YEAR

ESTACIONES DEL AÑO

spring	primavera
summer	verano
autumn, fall	otoño
winter	invierno

CUARTA PARTE

Verbos

CUARTA PARTE

REGULAR VERBS

REGULAR VERBS

VERBOS REGULARES

Lista de verbos regulares más importantes.

absorb	absorber
abuse	abusar, insultar
accept	aceptar
accommodate	acomodar
accompany	acompañar
accomplish	cumplir
ache	doler
acknowledge	reconocer
add	añadir
admire	admirar
adore	adorar
advance	adelantar
advertise	anunciar
affect	afectar
aid	ayudar
alternate	alternar
amuse	divertir
announce	anunciar
annoy	incomodar
answer	contestar
appeal	apelar
appreciate	apreciar
arrange	arreglar
arrest	arrestar
arrive	llegar
ask	preguntar
assist	asistir, ayudar
assure	asegurar

attempt	intentar
avoid	evitar
await	aguardar
bake	hornear
bathe	bañarse
behave	conducirse
believe	creer
belong	pertenecer
better	mejorar
bless	bendecir
boast	jactarse
boil	hervir
bother	fastidiar
breathe	respirar
brush	cepillar
burn	quemar
bury	enterrar
button	abotonar
call	llamar
carry	llevar
cease	cesar
challenge	desafiar
change	cambiar
chew	mascar
clean	limpiar
climb	trepar
close	cerrar
collect	cobrar
comb	peinar
command	mandar
comment	comentar
compare	comparar
complain	quejarse
compliment	piropear

confuse	confundir
correspond	corresponder
consent	consentir
consume	consumir
content	contentar
cook	cocinar
cough	toser
count	contar
cover	cubrir
cross	cruzar
crush	aplastar
cry	llorar
cure	curar
dance	bailar
dare	atreverse
darken	oscurecer
dawn	amanecer
deceive	engañar
decide	decidir
declare	declarar
decrease	disminuir
defeat	vencer
defend	defender
delay	dilatar
deliver	entregar
demonstrate	demostrar
deny	negar
deposit	depositar
descend	descender
deserve	merecer
desire	desear
destroy	destruir
develop	desarrollar
die	morir

differ	diferir
diminish	disminuir
direct	dirigir
dirty	ensuciar
disappear	desaparecer
disobey	desobedecer
distinguish	distinguir
distribute	distribuir
distrust	desconfiar
divide	dividir
doubt	dudar
dress	vestir
drizzle	lloviznar
drop	gotear
drown	ahogar
dry	secar
effect	efectuar
elect	elegir
embrace	abrazar
emit	emitir
employ	emplear
empty	vaciar
endure	sufrir
enjoy	disfrutar
enter	entrar
envy	envidiar
erase	borrar
escape	escapar
excuse	excusar
exercise	ejercitar
exhibit	exhibir
exist	existir
fail	fracasar
faint	desmayarse

fancy	imaginar
fear	temer
fill	llenar
finish	acabar
fire	disparar
fish	pescar
fix	fijar
fold	doblar
follow	seguir
free	libertar
fry	freir
gain	ganar
glitter	relucir
glue	encolar
govern	gobernar
grant	conceder
greet	saludar
hail	granizar
happen	acontecer
hate	aborrecer
heal	sanar
heat	calentar
help	ayudar
hunt	cazar
imitate	imitar
import	importar
improve	mejorar
include	incluir
increase	aumentar
infest	infestar
inform	informar
initiate	iniciar
innovate	innovar
inquire	averiguar

insist	insistir
inspire	inspirar
instruct	instruir
interpret	interpretar
interrogate	interrogar
interrupt	interrumpir
introduce	introducir
invent	inventar
iron	planchar
itch	picar
join	juntar
joke	bromear
judge	juzgar
jump	brincar
kick	patear
kill	matar
kiss	besar
lack	carecer
land	desembarcar
last	durar
laugh	reir
learn	aprender
lie	mentir
light	encender
like	gustar
limp	cojear
listen	escuchar
live	vivir
load	cargar
look	mirar
love	amar
maintain	mantener
manage	gobernar, administrar
match	parear

mediate	mediar
meditate	meditar
melt	derretir
milk	ordeñar
miss	echar de menos
mix	mezclar
molest	molestar
mount	montar
move	mover
multiply	multiplicar
nail	clavar
name	nombrar
need	necesitar
obey	obedecer
observe	observar
prepare	preparar
press	prensar
pretend	pretender
print	imprimir
proceed	proceder
produce	producir
prohibit	prohibir
project	proyectar
promise	prometer
propose	proponer
protest	protestar
prove	probar
provide	abastecer
publish	publicar
pull	halar
punish	castigar
push	empujar
rain	llover
raise	levantar

reach	alcanzar
recommend	recomendar
refer	referir
reflect	reflejar
refresh	refrescar
reign	reinar
rejoice	gozar
relate	relatar
relieve	aliviar
remain	permanecer
remember	acordarse
remove	remover
rent	arrendar
repeat	repetir
repel	rechazar
repent	arrepentirse
request	solicitar
resist	resistir
resolve	resolver
respect	respetar
rest	descansar
retire	retirar
return	volver
reward	recompensar
rock	mecer
roll	rodar
rule	gobernar
salt	salar
save	salvar
scratch	rascar
scream	chillar
seal	sellar
season	sazonar
separate	separar

serve	servir
settle	establecer
shake	sacudir
shame	avergonzar
shave	afeitar
ship	embarcar
show	mostrar
sigh	suspirar
sign	firmar
silence	enmudecer
sin	pecar
skate	patinar
sketch	bosquejar
slip	resbalar
smile	sonreir
smoke	fumar
sneeze	estornudar
snore	roncar
snow	nevar
solve	resolver
sound	sonar
spell	deletrear
spoil	estropear
sprinkle	rociar
squeeze	estrujar
stop	parar
study	estudiar
stumble	tropezar
suffer	sufrir
suggest	sugerir
supply	suministrar
support	apoyar
suppose	suponer
surprise	sorprender

suspect	sospechar
suspend	suspender
swallow	tragar
talk	hablar
taste	probar
tempt	tentar
thank	dar gracias
thunder	tronar
tie	atar
tire	cansar
toast	tostar
touch	tocar
trace	trazar
trade	comerciar
transfer	transferir
translate	traducir
travel	viajar
treat	tratar
tremble	temblar
trip	tropezar
trust	confiar
try	tratar
twist	torcer
unite	unir
use	usar
vary	variar
verify	comprobar
violate	violar
visit	visitar
wait	esperar
walk	andar, caminar
want	querer
wash	lavar
waste	desperdiciar

watch	vigilar
whisper	susurrar
wish	desear
wonder	maravillarse
work	trabajar

IRREGULAR VERBS

IRREGULAR VERBS

VERBOS IRREGULARES

Lista de verbos irregulares más importantes.

Presente		Pasado	Participio pasado
arise	levantarse	arose	arisen
awake	despertarse	awoke	awoken
be	ser, estar	was, were	been
beat	golpear	beat	beaten
become	llegar a ser	became	become
begin	comenzar	began	begun
bend	doblar	bent	bent
bet	apostar	bet	bet
bite	morder	bit	bitten
bleed	sangrar	bled	bled
blow	soplar	blew	blown
bring	traer	brought	brought
build	construir	built	built
buy	comprar	bought	bought
catch	coger	caught	caught
choose	escoger	chose	chosen
come	venir	came	come
cost	costar	cost	cost
cut	cortar	cut	cut
do	hacer	did	done
draw	dibujar	drew	drawn
drink	tomar	drank	drunk
drive	manejar	drove	driven
eat	comer	ate	eaten
fall	caer	fell	fallen
feed	alimentar	fed	fed

Presente		**Pasado**	**Participio pasado**
feel	sentir	felt	felt
fight	pelear	fought	fought
find	encontrar	found	found
fly	volar	flew	flown
forget	olvidar	forgot	forgotten
forgive	perdonar	forgave	forgiven
freeze	congelar	froze	frozen
get	obtener	got	gotten
give	dar	gave	given
go	ir	went	gone
grow	crecer	grew	grown
hang	colgar	hung	hung
have	tener	had	had
hear	oir	heard	heard
hide	esconder	hid	hidden
hit	golpear	hit	hit
hold	sostener	held	held
hurt	herir	hurt	hurt
keep	mantener	kept	kept
know	saber	knew	known
leave	salir	left	left
lend	prestar	lent	lent
let	permitir	let	let
light	iluminar	lit	lit
lose	perder	lost	lost
make	hacer	made	made
mean	querer decir	meant	meant
meet	conocer	met	met
pay	pagar	paid	paid
put	poner	put	put
read	leer	read	read
ride	montar	rode	ridden
ring	sonar	rang	rung
rise	subir	rose	risen

Presente		Pasado	Participio pasado
run	correr	ran	run
say	decir	said	said
see	ver	saw	seen
seek	buscar	sought	sought
sell	vender	sold	sold
send	enviar	sent	sent
set	colocar	set	set
shake	menear	shook	shaken
shine	brillar	shone	shone
shoot	disparar	shot	shot
show	mostrar	showed	shown
shut	cerrar	shut	shut
sing	cantar	sang	sung
sink	hundirse	sank	sunk
sit	sentarse	sat	sat
sleep	dormir	slept	slept
speak	hablar	spoke	spoken
spend	gastar	spent	spent
stand	levantarse	stood	stood
steal	robar	stole	stolen
swear	jurar	swore	sworn
sweep	barrer	swept	swept
swim	nadar	swam	swum
take	tomar, llevar	took	taken
teach	enseñar	taught	taught
tell	decir	told	told
think	pensar	thought	thought
throw	lanzar	threw	thrown
understand	entender	understood	understood
wake	despertar	woke	woken
wear	tener puesto	wore	worn
wet	mojar	wet	wet
win	ganar	won	won
write	escribir	wrote	written

QUINTA PARTE

Vocabulario

VOCABULARY

VOCABULARY

VOCABULARIO

Este vocabulario incluye todas las palabras usadas en este libro sin incluir las variaciones que se dan en ellas, ni el pasado y pasado participio de los verbos.

A

a	un, una
a lot of	mucho, muchos
about	acerca de, aproximadamente
above	sobre, encima de
absorb	absorber
abuse	abusar de
accept	aceptar
accident	accidente
accommodate	acomodar
accompany	acompañar
accomplish	realizar, lograr
accustom	acostumbrar
ache	dolor, doler
acknowledge	reconocer
across	a través de
act	acto, actuar
add	añadir
adjective	adjetivo
admire	admirar
admit	admitir
adore	adorar
advance	avanzar
adverb	adverbio
advertise	anunciar

afar	lejos
affect	afectar
affirmative	afirmativo
after	después de
afternoon	tarde
afterwards	después, posteriormente
again	otra vez
against	contra
ago	hace
ah!	¡ah!, ¡ay!
air	aire
airmail	correo aereo
airplane	avión
all	todo
almost	casi
aloud	fuerte, en voz alta
already	ya
also	también
alternate	alternar
although	aunque
always	siempre
am	soy, estoy
American	americano
among	entre
amuse	divertir
an	un, una
and	y, e
angry	airado, enojado
announce	anunciar
annoy	enojar
answer	respuesta, contestar
any	algún
anywhere	dondequiera
appeal	apelar, pedir ayuda

apple	manzana
appreciate	apreciar
April	abril
are	eres, estás, son, están
arise	elevarse, levantarse
around	alrededor, cerca
arrange	ordenar, arreglar
arrest	arrestar
arrive	llegar
article	artículo
artist	artista
as	tan, como
as…as	tan…como
not so…as	no tan…como
ask	preguntar, pedir
assist	asistir, ayudar
assure	asegurar
at	a, en
at last	al fin, por fin
attempt	intentar
August	agosto
autumn	otoño
auxiliary	auxiliar
avenue	avenida
avoid	evitar
await	esperar
awake	despertar
away	lejos
Away!	¡Fuera!

B

baby	bebe, niño
back	espalda, mover hacia atrás
be back	regresar
come back	volver
put back	devolver
backward	hacia atrás
bad	malo
bake	hornear
ball	bola
banana	plátano, guineo
baseball	beisbol, pelota
basic	básico
bath	baño
bathroom	cuarto de baño
be	ser, estar
be back	regresar
be hungry	tener hambre
beach	playa
beat	golpear
beautiful	hermoso
How beautiful!	¡Que hermosa!
because	porque
become	convertirse en
before	antes de
begin	comenzar
Begone!	¡Fuera!, ¡Vayase!
behave	comportarse
behind	detrás de
believe	creer
belong	pertenecer
below	abajo, debajo
bend	doblar

beneath	debajo, abajo
best	óptimo
bet	apuesta, apostar
better	mejor
between	en medio de
Beware!	¡Ten cuidado!
beyond	más allá
big	grande
bill	cuenta, billete
billion	billón
bite	morder
black	negro
bleed	sangrar
bless	bendecir
blow	soplar
blue	azul
boast	jactarse
boil	hervir
book	libro
bookstore	librería
boss	jefe
both	ambos
bother	molestar
bottle	botella
bottom	fondo
box	caja
boy	niño, muchacho
boyfriend	novio
Bravo!	¡Bravo!
Bread	pan
break	romper
breathe	respirar
briefcase	portafolio
bring	traer

brother	hermano
brown	marrón
brush	cepillo, cepillar
build	construir
building	edificio
burn	quemar
bury	enterrar
bus	autobús
busy	ocupado
but	pero
not only…but	no sólo…pero
button	botón, abotonar
buy	comprar
by	por

C

cafeteria	cafetería
calendar	calendario
call	llamada, llamar
can	poder
candy	dulce
capital	capital
car	automóvil, carro
careful	cuidadoso
careless	descuidado
carry	llevar, sostener
case	caso
cashier	cajero
cat	gato
catch	atrapar, agarrar
cease	cesar
chair	silla
challenge	desafiar

change	cambiar
chase	cazar, perseguir
cheap	barato
cheer	alegría
Cheer up!	¡Ánimo!
chew	masticar
child	niño
children	niños
choose	escoger
church	iglesia
cigar	cigarro
cigarette	cigarrillo
class	clase
classroom	salón de clase
clean	limpio, limpiar
clever	inteligente
climb	escalar, subir
clock	reloj
close	cerrar
clothes	ropa
cloud	nube
coal	carbón
coat	chaqueta, abrigo
coffee	café
cold	frío
collect	coleccionar, cobrar
college	colegio
comb	peine, peinar
come	venir
come back	volver
come in	entrar
comfortable	cómodo
command	ordenar, mandar
comment	comentario, comentar

communication	comunicación
compare	comparar
complain	quejarse
compliment	elogio, halagar
composition	composición
computer	computadora
conditional	condicional
confuse	confundir
conjunction	conjunción
consent	consentir
consume	consumir
content	contenido
contract	contrato, contratar
contraction	contracción
cook	cocinero, cocinar
cookie	galleta
corner	esquina
correct	correcto, corregir
correspond	corresponder
cost	costo, costar
couch	sofa, mueble
cough	tos, toser
could	podría, pasado de can
count	contar
course	curso
cousin	primo, prima
cover	cubrir
cross	cruz, cruzar
crush	majar, aplastar
cry	gritar, llorar
cure	cura, curar
cut	cortar

D

daily	diariamente
dance	bailar
dare	desafiar
dark	oscuro
darken	oscurecer
daughter	hija
dawn	alba, amanecer
day	día
a day	al día
deceive	engañar
December	diciembre
decide	decidir
declare	declarar
decrease	reducir, disminuir
defeat	derrotar
defend	defender
definite	definido
degree	grado
delay	delatar, tardar
deliver	entregar, repartir
demonstrate	demostrar
dentist	dentista
deny	negar
deposit	depósito, depositar
descend	descender
deserve	merecer
desire	deseo, desear
desk	escritorio
dessert	postre, dulces
destroy	destruir
develop	desarrollar

die	morir
differ	diferir
difficult	difícil
diminish	disminuir
dining room	comedor
dinner	cena
direct	directo, dirigir
dirty	sucio, ensuciar
disappear	desaparecer
dish	plato
disobey	desobedecer
distinguish	distinguir
distribute	distribuir
distrust	desconfiado, desconfiar
divide	dividir
do	hacer
doctor	doctor
dog	perro
dollar	dólar
Dominican	dominicano
door	puerta
doubt	duda, dudar
draw	dibujar
drawer	gaveta, cajón
dress	vestido, vestir
drink	bebida, beber
drive	conducir, guiar
drizzle	llovizna, lloviznar
drop	gota, dejar caer
drown	ahogar
dry	seco, secar
during	durante

E

each	cada
each other	uno a otro
early	temprano
easy	fácil
eat	comer
effect	efecto, efectuar
egg	huevo
eight	ocho
eighteen	dieciocho
eighteenth	decimoctavo
eighth	octavo
eightieth	octogésimo
eighty	ochenta
either...or	o...o
elect	electo, elegir
elephant	elefante
eleven	once
eleventh	undécimo
elsewhere	en otra parte
embrace	abrazo, abrazar
emit	emitir
employ	empleo, emplear
empty	vacio, vaciar
endure	sufrir, soportar
English	inglés
enjoy	gozar de, disfrutar de
enough	bastante, suficiente
enter	entrar, ingresar
entire	entero
entirely	enteramente
envy	envidia, envidiar
erase	borrar

eraser	borrador
escape	huida, escaparse
even	aún, nivelado
ever	siempre, alguna vez
every	cada, todos
everybody	todos
everywhere	en todas partes
example	ejemplo
except	excepto, excluir
exceptional	exceptional
excuse	excusa, excusar
exercise	ejercicio, ejercitar
exhibit	exhibir
exist	existir
expensive	costoso, caro
experience	experiencia
explain	explicar

F

factory	fabrica, taller
fail	faltar, fallar
faint	débil, desmayarse
faithful	fiel
fall	otoño, caer
family	familia
fancy	fantasía, fino
far	lejos
fast	rápido, ayunar
father	padre
favor	favor
in favor of	a favor de
fear	miedo, temer
February	febrero

feed	alimentar
feel	sentir
feet	pies
fence	empalizada, cercar
few	pocos
fifteen	quince
fifteenth	decimoquinto
fifth	quinto
fiftieth	quincuagésimo
fifty	cincuenta
fight	pelear
fill	llenar
find	encontrar
fine	bién, excelente
finger	dedo
finish	terminar
fire	fuego, encender, despedir
first	primero
fish	pescado, pescar
five	cinco
fix	arreglar, fijar
flashy	llamativo
floor	piso
flower	flor, florecer
fly	volar
fold	doblar
follow	seguir
foolish	tonto
foot	pie
on foot	a pie
for	para, por
forever	siempre, para siempre
forget	olvidar
forgive	perdonar

form	forma, formulario, formar
fortieth	cuadragésimo
forty	cuarenta
Forward!	¡Adelante!
four	cuatro
fourteen	catorce
fourteenth	decimocuarto
fourth	cuarto
France	Francia
free	libre, gratis, libertar
freeze	congelar
French	Francés
frequent	frecuente
frequently	frecuentemente
Friday	viernes
from	de, desde
fry	fritura, freír

G

gain	ganancia, ganar
gallon	galón
game	juego
garden	jardín
German	Alemán
get	obtener, recibir
get married	casarse
Get Out!	¡Fuera!
get up	levantarse
girl	muchacha
girlfriend	novia, amiga
give	dar
glass	vidrio, vaso
glitter	brillo, brillar

glue	cola, pegar
go	ir
go back	regresar
go in	entrar
go out	salir
good	bueno
Good Heavens!	¡Santo Cielo!
Govern	gobernar
grammar	gramática
grant	donación, otorgar
grass	hierba
green	verde
greet	saludar
grocery	bodega, colmado
group	grupo, agrupar
grow	crecer
guest	visita, huesped

H

hail	grito, aclamar
hair	pelo, cabello
ham	jamón
hand	mano
hang	colgar
happen	suceder
happy	feliz
hard	duro, difícil
has	tiene
hat	sombrero
hate	odio, odiar
have	tener, haber
have a good time	divertirse
have to	tener que

he	él
headache	dolor de cabeza
heal	sanar
healthy	saludable
hear	oir, escuchar
heat	calor, calentar
heaven	cielo
Good Heavens!	¡Santo Cielo!
heavy	pesado
Hello!	¡Hola!
help	ayuda, ayudar
her	su, sus (de ella), a ella, la
here	aquí
Look Here!	¡Mire!
herself	ella misma
hide	esconder
high	alto
him	a él, le
himself	él mismo
his	su, sus (de él)
History	Historia
hit	éxito, golpear, pegar
hold	agarrar, sujetar
hole	hoyo, pozo
holiday	día de fiesta, vacaciones
home	casa, hagar
homework	tarea
honest	honrado, honesto
horse	caballo
hospital	hospital
hour	hora
house	casa, alojar
how	cómo
How Beautiful!	¡Que Hermosa!

How many?	¿Cuántos?
How much?	¿Cuánto?
however	sin embargo
hundred	cien
one hundred	
thousand	cien mil
hundredth	centésimo
hunger	hambre
hungry	hambriento
be hungry	tener hambre
hurry	apresurarse
hurt	herir, lastimar

I

I	yo
ice	hielo, enfriar
ice cream	helado
idea	idea
if	si
ill	enfermo, mal
imitate	imitar
immediate	inmediato
imperative	imperativo
import	importar
important	importante
improve	mejorar
in	en
include	incluir
increase	aumento, aumentar
Indeed!	¡De Veras! ¡Claro!
Indefinite	indefinido
infest	infestar
inform	informar

information	informacíon, informativo
initiate	iniciar
innovate	innovar
inquire	preguantar, investigar
insist	insistir
inspire	inspirar
instant	instante
instruct	instruir
intelligent	inteligente
interesting	interesante
interjection	interjección
international	internacional
interpret	interpretar
interrogate	interrogar
interrupt	interrumpir
into	en, dentro de
introduce	introducir, presentar
invent	inventar
iron	hierro, planchar
irregular	irregular
is	es, está
island	isla
it	ello
itch	picar
its	su, sus, (de animal o cosa)
itself	el mismo, la misma

J

jail	cárcel, encarcelar
January	enero
job	trabajo, empleo
join	juntar, ingresar
joke	broma, chiste

judge	juez, juzgar
juice	jugo
July	julio
jump	salto, saltar
June	junio

K

keep	guardar, mantener
key	llave, clave
kick	patada, patear
kill	matar
kind	clase, bondadoso
kindness	bondad
kiss	beso, besar
kitchen	cocina
knife	cuchillo, acuchillar
knock	golpear, pegar
know	saber, conocer

L

lack	escasez, carecer de
lady	dama
land	tierra, aterrizar
language	idioma
large	grande
last	pasado, durar
late	tarde, atrasado
later	luego, más tarde
laugh	risa, reir
lawyer	abogado
learn	aprender
lemon	limón

lemonade	limonada
lend	prestar
less	menos
lesson	lección
lest	no sea que, a no ser que
let	permitir, dejar
letter	carta, letra
library	biblioteca
lie	acostarse, mentir
lieutenant	teniente
life	vida
light	claro, luz, iluminar
like	como, gustar
limp	cojear
listen to	escuchar
little	pequeño, poco
live	vivir
long	largo, mucho tiempo
How long?	¿Cuánto tiempo?
look	mirar, parecer
look at	mirar
Look Here!	¡Mire!
Look Out!	¡Cuidado!
lose	perder
lot	gran cantidad
a lot of	mucho, muchos
love	amor, amar, querer
lunch	almuerzo, almorzar

M

magazine	revista
maid	criada, sirvienta
mail	correspondencia, enviar por correo

mailman	cartero
maintain	mantener
make	hacer
man	hombre
manage	dirigir, administrar
many	muchos
March	marzo, marchar
mark	marca, marcar
marry	casarse
match	pareja, unir
mathematics	matemática
matter	asunto, materia, importar
May	mayo
may	poder
me	mi
meal	comida
mean	significar, querer decir
meat	carne
mechanic	mecánico
mediate	mediar
meet	conocer, encontrarse con, reunirse
melt	derretir
men	hombres
message	mensaje
mice	ratones
middle	medio, intermedio
million	millón
mind	mente
Never Mind!	¡No Importa!
mine	el mío, mina, minar
minute	minuto, momento
mirror	espejo
Miss	Señorita
miss	echar de menos, perder

mistake	error, equivocarse
mix	mezcla, mezclar
mode	modo, manera
molest	molestia, molestar
moment	momento
Monday	lunes
money	dinero
month	mes
more	más
morning	mañana
most	la mayor parte
mostly	esencialmente, mayormente
mother	madre
mount	montar, ascender
mountain	montaña
mouse	ratón
move	movimiento, mover
movies	cine
Mr.	señor
Mrs.	Señora
much	mucho
multipy	multiplicar
must	deber, tener que
my	mi, mis
myself	yo mismo

N

nail	uña, clavo, clavar
name	nombre, nombrar
nationality	nacionalidad
near	cerca de
nearly	casi
necessary	necesario

need	necesidad, necesitar
negative	negativo
neither	negativo
neither…nor	ni…ni
never	nunca
Never Mind!	¡No Importa!
nevertheless	sin embargo
new	nuevo
newspaper	periódico
next	próximo
nice	lindo, delicado
night	noche
nightclub	club nocturno, sala de fiestas
nine	nueve
nineteen	diecinueve
ninetieth	nonagésimo
ninety	noventa
ninth	noveno
no	no, ninguno
nobody	nadie
Nonsense!	¡Tontería!
noon	mediodía
nor	ni
not	no
not only…but	no solo…pero
not so…as	no tan…como
notebook	libreta, cuaderno
now	ahora, ya
right now	ahora mismo
nowhere	en ninguna parte
number	número, numerar
nurse	enfermero

O

obey	obedecer
objective	objetivo
objective case	caso acusativo
observe	observar
ocean	océano
o'clock	en punto
October	octubre
of	de
off	fuera de
office	oficina
often	a menudo
oil	aceite
on	en, encima de
once	una vez
one	uno
only	solamente
not only…but	no solo…pero
open	abierto, abrir
orange	naranja, anaranjado
order	orden, ordenar
other	otro
each other	uno a otro
Ouch!	¡Huy! ¡Ay!
our	nuestro
ours	el nuestro
ourselves	nosotros mismos
out	fuera
over	sobre, encima de
over there	ahí, allá, allí

P

pacific	pacífico
package	paquete, empacar
page	página, paginar
paint	pintura, pintar
painting	pintura
pair	par, parear
paper	papel, empapelar
parent	padre
park	parque, estacionar
party	fiesta, partido
pass	pase, pasar
passive	pasivo
past	pasado
pay	paga, pagar
pay attention	poner atención
peaceful	pacífico, tanquilo
pen	lapicero, pluma
pencil	lápiz
people	pueblo, gente, poblar
pepper	pimienta
perfect	perfecto, perfeccionar
personal	personal
phone	teléfono
piano	piano
pick	pico
pick up	recoger, levantar
picture	cuadro, pintura, retrato
piece	pedazo, pieza
pilot	piloto, pilotar
pink	rosado
pity	compasión, lástima
What A Pity!	¡Que Lástima!

place	lugar, colocar
plan	proyecto, planear
plane	avión
plate	plato
play	jugar, tocar
please	por favor, gustar
plural	plural
pocket	bolsillo, embolsillar
police	policía
policeman	policía
policemen	policías
poor	pobre
porch	pórtico, galería
possessive	posesivo
potato	papa
pound	libra
practice	práctica, practicar
prepare	preparar
present	presente, regalo, presentar, regalar
president	presidente
press	prensa, apretar
pretend	pretender, simular
pretty	bonito, bastante
previous	previo, anterior
price	precio, preciar
print	impresión, imprimir
problem	problema
proceed	proseguir, seguir
produce	producir
professional	profesional
program	programa, programar
progress	progreso, progresar, adelantar
progressive	progresivo
prohibit	prohibir

project	proyecto, proyectar
promise	promesa, prometer
pronoun	pronombre
propose	proponer, sugerir
protest	protesta, protestar
prove	probar
provide	proveer, suministrar
Pshaw!	¡Bah!
publish	publicar
pull	tirón, halar
punish	castigar
puppy	cachorro, cachorrito
purse	bolsa, cartera
push	empujar
put	poner

Q

quantity	cantidad
question	preguanta, preguantar
quick	rápido

R

radio	radio, radiodifundir
rain	lluvia, llover
raise	levantar
reach	alcanzar
read	leer
ready	listo, preparado, preparar
real	real, verdadero
Really!	¡Es Verdad!, ¡De Veras!
receive	recibir
recommend	recomendar

refer	referir
reflect	reflejar, reflexionar
reflexive	reflexivo
refresh	refresco, refrescar
regarding	respecto a
regular	regular
reign	reino, reinar
rejoice	alegría, regocijarse
relate	relacionar
remain	permanecer
remember	recordar
remove	remover
rent	renta, alquiler, alquilar
repeat	repetir
repel	rechazar
repent	arrepentirse
request	ruego, solicitud, solicitar
resist	resistir, oponerse
resolve	resolver
respect	respetar
rest	descanso, descansar
restaurant	restaurante
retire	retirar, retirarse
return	regresar
reward	premio, premiar
rice	arroz, desmenuzar
ride	paseo, montar
rifle	rifle, fusíl, robar
right	recto, correcto, derecho
right now	ahora mismo
ring	anillo, sonar
rise	subir, levantarse
river	río
road	camino

rock	roca, piedra
roll	rollo, rodar, girar
room	habitación
round	redondo, alrededor, redondearse
rug	alfombra
rule	regla, gobernar
run	carrera, correr
Russian	Ruso

S

salt	sal, salar
same	mismo
sandwich	emparedado
Saturday	sábado
sauce	salsa
save	salvo, salvar, ahorrar
say	decir
scarce	escaso, insuficiente
scarcely	apenas, escasamente
school	escuela, instruir
sea	mar
seal	foca, sello, sellar
seat	asiento, acomodar
second	segundo, secundar, apoyar
secretary	secretario
see	ver
seek	buscar
seem	parecer
seldom	raramente, pocas veces
sell	vender
send	enviar
sentence	oración, frase, sentenciar
separate	separar

September	septiembre
serious	serio, grave
serve	servir
set	juego, colocar
settle	arreglar, establecerse
seven	siete
seventeen	diecisiete
seventeenth	decimoséptimo
seventh	séptimo
seventieth	septuagésimo
seventy	setenta
several	varios
shake	sacudir
shame	verguenza, lástima, avergonzar
shave	resurar, afeitar
she	ella
shine	brillo, brillar
ship	barco, embarcar, enviar
shirt	camisa
shoe	zapato
shoot	disparar, tirar
should	debiera, debería
shout	gritar,vocear
show	espectáculo, mostrar, exhibir
shut	cerrar, tapar
sick	enfermo
sigh	suspiro, suspirar
silence	silencio, hacer callar
simple	simple, fácil
sin	pecado, pecar
since	desde, puesto que, ya que
sincere	sincero
sing	cantar
sink	fregadero, sumergirse, descender

sister	hermana
sit	sentarse
sit down	sentarse
six	seis
sixteen	dieciséis
sixteenth	decimosexto
sixth	sexto
sixtieth	sexagésimo
sixty	sesenta
skate	patín, patinar
sketch	boceto, bosquejar
skirt	falda, bordear
sky	cielo
sleep	sueño, dormir
slip	resbalar, deslizarse
slow	lento, despacio, retardar
small	pequeño
smile	sonrisa, sonreir
smoke	humo, humer, fumar
sneeze	estornudo, estornudar
snore	ronquido, roncar
snow	nieve, nevar
so	así, tan
so that	para que, de modo que
not so…as	no…tan como
soft	suave, blando
soldier	soldado, militar
solve	resolver
some	algún, algunos, un poco de
somebody	alguien
someone	alguien
something	algo
sometime	alguna vez
sometimes	a veces

somewhere	en alguna parte
son	hijo
song	canción, canto
soon	pronto
sound	sonido, sonar, tocar
soup	sopa
sour	agrio, ácido
Spanish	español
speak	hablar
speech	discurso
spell	hechizo, deletrear
spend	gastar, pasar (tiempo)
spoil	dañar, malcriar
spring	primavera
sprinkle	rociar, lloviznar
squeeze	apretar, exprimir
stand	pararse
stand up	pararse, levantarse
state	estado, declarar
steal	robar
still	quieto, todavía, calmar
stop	parada, parar
store	tienda, acumular
story	cuento, piso, historiar
stove	estufa
strange	extraño, raro
strict	estricto, puntual
strong	fuerte, poderoso
student	estudiante
study	estudio, estudiar
stumble	tropezón, tropezar, titubear
sudden	súbito, repentino
suddenly	de repente
suffer	sufrir

sugar	azúcar, azucarar
suggest	sugerir
sun	sol, solear
Sunday	domingo
superlative	superlativo
supper	cena
supply	suministro, suministrar
support	apoyo, apoyar
suppose	suponer, imaginar
sure	seguro, cierto
surprise	sorpresa, sorprender
suspect	sospechoso, sospechar
suspend	suspender
swallow	trago, tragar
swear	jurar
sweet	dulce, dulzura
swim	baño, nadar

T

table	mesa, colocar en la mesa
tail	cola, perseguir
take	tomar, llevar
talk	hablar
tall	alto
taste	gusto, sabor, probar
taxi	táxi
tea	té
teach	enseñar
teacher	maestro, profesor
teeth	dientes
telephone	teléfono
television	televisión
television set	televisor

tell	decir, contar
tempt	tentar
ten	diez
tennis	tenis
tense	tenso, tiempo (gramatical), ponerse tenso
tenth	décimo
test	exámen, examinar
than	que
thank	agradecer
that	ese, aquél, que
the	el, la, los, las
their	su, sus (de ellos)
theirs	suyo (de ellos)
them	les, a ellos
themselves	ellos mismos
there	allí, allá
there is	hay (singular)
there are	hay (plural)
these	estos, estas
they	ellos, ellas
thing	cosa, objeto
think	pensar, creer
third	tercero
thirsty	sediento
be thirsty	tener sed
thirteen	trece
thirtieth	trigésimo
thirty	treinta
this	esto, esta
those	esos, esas
though	aunque
thousand	mil
thousandth	milésimo

three	tres
throw	tirar, lanzar
thunder	trueno, tronar
Thursday	jueves
thus	así, de este modo
tie	atar, amarrar
till	hasta
time	tiempo, hora, momento
at times	a veces
on time	a tiempo
tire	neumático, cansarse
tired	cansado
to	a, hacia, para
toast	tostada, tostar
today	hoy
together	juntos
tomato	tomate
tomorrow	mañana
tonight	esta noche
too	también, demasiado
too much	demasiado
tooth	diente
touch	toque, tacto, tocar
town	pueblo, municipio
toy	juguete
trace	rastro, huella, rastrear, investigar
trade	comercio, negocio
train	tren, entrenar
transfer	transferir
translate	traducir
travel	viaje, viajar
treat	tratar
tremble	temblor, temblar

trip	viaje, tropezar
true	verdadero, leal
truly	sinceramente, verdaderamente
trust	confianza, confiar
truth	verdad
try	prueba, tratar, intentar, probar
trying	molesto, penoso, duro
Tuesday	martes
turn	doblar, girar
turn on	encender, prender
T.V.	televisión
twelfth	duodécimo
twelve	doce
twentieth	vigésimo
twenty	veinte
twice	dos veces
twist	girar, dar vueltas
type	tipo, clasificar, escribir a máquina

U

umbrella	paraguas, sombrilla
understand	comprender, entender
unite	unir
United States of America	Estados Unidos de América
university	universidad, universitario
unless	a menos que
until	hasta
up	arriba
Cheer Up!	¡Animo!
upward	hacia arriba

us	nos, nosotros
use	uso, usar
useful	útil
usual	usual, común

V

vacation	vacación
vary	variar
verb	verbo
verify	verificar
very	muy
violate	violar
violin	violín
visit	visita, visitar
voice	voz, proclamar

W

wait	espera, esperar
wait for	esperar a
waiter	camarero, mozo
waitress	camarera, moza
wake	vigilia, vela, despertar
walk	paseo, caminata, andar, caminar
wall	pared, muro, emparedar, amurallar
wallet	cartera
want	deseo, desear
war	guerra, guerrear
warm	caliente, calentar
was	era, estaba
wash	lavar
watch	reloj, mirar, vigilar
water	agua, mojar

we	nosotros
weak	débil
wear	usar, llevar puesto
weather	tiempo (atmosférico)
week	semana
a week	a la semana
Welcome!	¡Bienvenido!
well	bién, pozo
were	era, estaba
wet	mojado, humedecer
what	qué, lo que
What A Pity!	¡Que Lastima!
when	cuándo
whenever	cuando quiera
where	dónde
whereas	puesto que
whether	si
whether…or	sea que…o, si…o
while	rato, mientras que
whisper	susurro, susurrar
white	blanco, blanquear
who	quién, que
whole	entero, todo
why	por qué
wide	ancho
will	voluntad, auxiliar del futuro
win	ganar
window	ventana
wine	vino, beber vino
winter	invierno, invernar
wish	deseo, desear
with	con
woman	mujer
women	mujeres

wonder	admiración, maravilla, maravillarse, preguantarse
word	palabra, expresar en palabras
work	trabajo, empleo, trabajar, emplear
workman	obrero, trabajador
workmen	obreros, trabajadores
world	mundo, mundial

Y

yard	patio
year	año
yellow	amarillo, yema de huevo, ponerse amarillo
yesterday	ayer
yet	aún, todavía
you	tú, usted, ustedes
young	joven
your	tu, su
yours	tuyo, suyo
yourself	tú mismo, usted mismo
yourselves	ustedes mismos

Z

zero	cero, nulo

PROPER NOUNS

PROPER NOUNS

NOMBRES PROPIOS

A continuación damos los nombres de personas, paises y ciudades que hemos usado en este libro.

America
United States of America
Arias
Mr. Arias
Bani
Benjamin
Benny
Betty
Bill
Bob
Boston
Brazil
Brown
Mr. Brown
Canada
Chicago
Christopher
Clark
President Clark
Clinton
Mr. Clinton
Duarte
Duarte Street
Elizabeth
England
Enmanuel
Erik

Europe

Frank

Franklin

George

Green

  Mr. Green

Helen

Henry

Hull

  Secretary Hull

Janet

Jenny

John

Johnson

  Lieutenant Johnson

Joseph

Kathy

Kelvin

Lara

  Miss Lara

  Mr. Lara

Linda

Lisa

London

Lopez

  Mr. Lopez

Lucy

Margaret

Mark

Mary

Mexico

Miami

Michael

New York

Ocoa
Paul
Peter
Rafael
Ramirez
   Mr. Ramirez
   Mrs. Ramirez
Robert
Rodriguez
   Miss Rodriguez
Sanchez
   Mr. Sanchez
Santiago
Santo Domingo
Silver
   Mrs. Silver
Smith
   Miss Smith
   Mr. Smith
Suzan
Tom
Tommy
United States of America
Venecia
Washington
   Washington Avenue
White
   Mr. White
   Mrs. White
William

BIBLIOGRAFIA

BIBLIOGRAFIA

THE OXFORD GUIDE TO ENGLISH USAGE
  The Essential Guide to Correct English
  Compiled by Edmund Weiner and Andrew Delahunty
  Oxford University Press, 1994

GRAMMAR IN USE
  Reference and Practice for intermediate Students of English
  Raymon Murphy with Roann Altman
  Consultant: William E. Rutherford
  Cambridge University Press, 1990

UNDERSTANDING AND USING ENGLISH GRAMMAR
  Betty Schrampfer Azar
  Regents/Prentice Hall, Inc., 1989,

THE BANTAM NEW COLLEGE REVISED SPANISH & ENGLISH DICTIONARY
  Edwin B. Williams, Professor of Romance Languages
  University of Pennsylvania
  Bantam Books, 1987

THE UNIVERSITY OF CHICAGO SPANISH-ENGLISH AND ENGLISH-SPANISH DICTIONARY
  Carlos Castillo and Otto F. Bond
  With the Assistance of Barbara M. Garcia
  Revised and Enlarged by D. Lincoln Canfield
  Pocket Books, Simon & Schuster, Inc.
  The University of Chicago, 1987.

PEQUEÑO LAROUSSE ILUSTRADO
  Ramón García-Pelayo y Gross
  Ediciones Larousse, México, D.F., 1987

REGENTS ENGLISH WORKBOOK, BOOK 3
  Robert J. Dixson
  Regents Publishing Company, Inc., 1986

SECOND BOOK IN ENGLISH
  A New Revised Edition
  Robert J. Dixson
  Regents Publishing Company, Inc., 1983

METODO CORTINA, INGLÉS EN 20 LECCIONES
  R. Diez de la Cortina
  Revisado por Manuel Duran
  Cortina Learning International, Inc., 1977.

Prof. Benjamin Franklin Arias, Ph.D.

ENGLISH SENTENCE STRUCTURE
   The Succesor to English Sentence Patterns
   Robert Krohn and the Staff of the English Language Institute
   Ann Arbor, The University of Michigan Press, 1975.

BEGINNING LESSONS IN ENGLISH
   A New Revised Edition
   Isobel Yealy Fisher and Robert J. Dixson
   Regents Publishing Company, Inc., 1971.

THE NEW WORLD SPANISH/ENGLISH AND ENGLISH/SPANISH DICTIONARY
   Prepared under the Supervision of Mario A. Pei, Professor of Romance
   Philology
   Columbia University
   Editor, Salvatore Ramondino
   New American Library, 1968

RESUMEN PRACTICO DE LA GRAMATICA INGLESA
   Robert J. Dixson y Julio I Andujar
   Regents Publishing Company, 1967.

METODO DE INGLÉS
   Juan Marín Aguilu
   The Marin School of Languages
   New York, U.S.A.
   Compañía Bibliografica Española, S.A., 1963

LEARNING AMERICAN ENGLISH
   Grant Taylor
   McGraw-Hill Book Company, Inc., 1956

MASTERING AMERICAN ENGLISH
   International Student Edition
   Grant Taylor
   McGraw-Hill Book Company, Inc., 1956

REGENTS ENGLISH WORKBOOK, BOOKS 1AND 2
   Robert J. Dixson
   Regents Publishing Company, Inc., 1956.

OTROS LIBROS DEL AUTOR

AGENDA BIBLICA
CON UNA GUIA DE LECTURAS DIARIAS
Por Benjamín Franklin Arias, Ph.D.
benfrank1305@gmail.com

Te ayuda a disciplinarte para leer la Biblia cada día y completa cada año siguiendo la Guía de Lecturas Diarias. Tiene espacio para escribir las citas y actividades programadas o para pensamientos, reflexiones y meditaciones basadas en la lectura correspondiente.

Format: Perfect Bound Softcover (B/W)
ISBN: 9781426934834

Format: E-Book
ISBN: 9781426934841

www.trafford.com

GRANDES ENSEÑANZAS
EN MENSAJES PEQUEÑOS
Por Benjamín Franklin Arias, Ph.D.
benfrank1305@gmail.com

Un libro con dos Artículos Educativos para cada mes
y Frases Célebres para cada día del año.

Format: Perfect Bound Softcover (B/W)
ISBN: 9781490788616

Format: E-Book
ISBN: 97814907886

www.trafford.com

ARTICULOS Y CRUCIGRAMAS EDUCATIVOS
PARA TODA LA FAMILIA
Por Benjamín Franklin Arias, Ph.D.
benfrank1305@gmail.com

Un libro con 40 Artículos Educativos de temas variados y 40 Crucigramas para el entretenimiento de toda la familia, para aprender de todo un poco.

Format: Perfect Bound Softcover (B/W)
ISBN: 9781698703510

Format: E-Book
ISBN: 9781698703503

www.trafford.com

SABIDURIA INTEGRAL
PARA EL DESARROLLO PERSONAL
Por Benjamín Franklin Arias, Ph.D.
benfrank1305@gmail.com

Un libro con 70 artículos de temas variados que te pueden ayudar en tu desarrollo personal. Divido en 10 secciones con 7 temas interesantes cada una.

Format: Perfect Bound Softcover (B/W)
ISBN: 9781698705491

Format: E-Book
ISBN: 9781698705484

www.trafford.com

CRUCIGRAMAS
PARA EL TIEMPO LIBRE
Por Benjamin Franklin Arias, Ph.D.
benfrank1305@gmail.com

Una colección de 70 Crucigramas que anteriormente fueron publicados por el autor en diferentes periódicos de República Dominicana y de Estados Unidos.

Format: Softcover (B/W)
ISBN: 9781698708430

Format: E-Book
ISBN: 9781698708423

www.trafford.com